PSYCHOLOGY

FOR

TRAINERS

Alison Hardingham

Alison Hardingham read experimental psychology at Oxford University. Her career in education, human factors, and business psychology has brought her into contact with all kinds of teaching and training. She has designed and delivered a huge variety of programmes, from one-to-one tuition with psychotic children to teambuilding with senior managers, and from basic maths with a class of disaffected adolescents to interviewing skills with engineers. She is the director of consultancy services at Interactive Skills, a human resource consultancy which specialises in management development, assessment, and organisational development. She has written many books on psychology, personal effectiveness, and HR issues. Her books include *Pulling Together: Teamwork in practice* (1994), co-authored with Jenny Royal, *Working in Teams* (1995), and, in this series, *Designing Training* (1996), all published by the IPD. With Charlotte Ellis, she is the author of a trainers' toolkit, *Exercises for Team Development*, also published by the IPD. She lives in Oxfordshire with her son, Ian. She believes in experiencing training as well as providing it to others, and so has recently taken up scuba-diving and playing the saxophone.

In the TRAINING ESSENTIALS series leading experts focus on the key issues in contemporary training. The books are thoroughly comprehensive, setting out the theoretical background while also providing practical guidance to meet the 'hands-on' needs of training practitioners. They are essential reading for trainers and for students working towards training qualifications – N/SVQs, and Diploma and Certificate courses in training and development.

Other titles in the series include:

Creating a Training and Development Strategy Andrew Mayo

Cultivating Self-Development David Megginson and Vivien Whitaker

Delivering Training Suzy Siddons

Designing Training Alison Hardingham

Developing Learning Materials Jacqui Gough

Evaluating Training Peter Bramley

Facilitation Skills Frances and Roland Bee

Identifying Training Needs Tom Boydell and Malcolm Leary

Introduction to Training Penny Hackett

The Institute of Personnel and Development is the leading publisher of books and reports for personnel and training professionals, students, and all those concerned with the effective management and development of people at work. For full details of all our titles please telephone the Publishing Department:

tel. 0181-263 3387
fax 0181-263 3850
e-mail publish@ipd.co.uk

The catalogue of all IPD titles can be viewed on the IPD website:
www.ipd.co.uk

TRAINING ESSENTIALS

PSYCHOLOGY

FOR

TRAINERS

Alison Hardingham

INSTITUTE OF PERSONNEL AND DEVELOPMENT

First published in 1998
Reprinted 1999

Design and typesetting by Paperweight
Printed in Great Britain by
The Cromwell Press, Wiltshire

British Library Cataloguing in Publication Data
A catalogue record for this book is available from the
British Library

ISBN
0-85292-681-2

INSTITUTE OF PERSONNEL
AND DEVELOPMENT

IPD House, Camp Road, London SW19 4UX
Tel.: 0181 971 9000   Fax: 0181 263 3333
Registered office as above. Registered Charity No. 1038333.
A company limited by guarantee. Registered in England No. 2931892.

Contents

Acknowledgements		vi
1	Why 'Psychology for Trainers'?	1
2	Building Rapport, Establishing Credibility	9
3	Getting Information Across	35
4	Commitment to Change	53
5	Managing the Group	72
6	Counselling the Individual	93
7	Handling Conflict	114
8	Facilitating Transfer of Learning	135
9	Surviving as a Trainer	152
Conclusion		168
References and Further Reading		170
Index		172

Acknowledgements

I should like to dedicate this book to the people whose encouragement, support and generosity made it possible for me to write it: to Anne Cordwent, my commissioning editor; to Jackie, my secretary; and to all my colleagues and friends at Interactive Skills, most especially Julia, Jenny, Nicky and Rob.

Why 'Psychology for Trainers'?

'Trainers need psychology like a fish needs a bicycle': true or false?

What would a training programme designed in complete ignorance of human psychology be like? Maybe something like this…

The 29 participants filed one by one into the windowless room. At the front stood the trainer, behind a dark oak lectern. The tables were in lines across the room, and name cards indicated who was to sit where. At each place was a thick file full of dense typescript. On the front of the file was the title of the training course the participants were about to receive: 'The basic management skills'. The course was to last five days.

The trainer waited until everyone was seated. Then she started:

'Good morning, ladies and gentlemen, and welcome to this programme in basic management skills. I shall be describing the 10 main theories of management and indicating the strengths and limitations of each. You may think you already know the basics of management, but I can assure you plenty of managers make elementary mistakes all the time. That is why this programme has been designed.

Now, if you would turn to page 32(a) of your file, we will begin with the origins and development of the situational leadership model. The list of points that I have put up on the overhead shows you...'

And so on.

How many 'deliberate mistakes' did you spot in that happily fictitious account? Here are some you may have noticed:

▮ '29 participants'	a prime number, difficult for pairs, trios, or group work
▮ 'windowless room'	no light, no contact with the outside world
▮ 'trainer...behind a dark oak lectern'	a message of distance and inaccessibility
▮ 'the basic management skills'	a title at best uninspiring, at worst insulting
▮ '10 main theories'	far too many for people to take in or remember
▮ 'I can assure you'	patronising tone
▮ 'the list of points'	no diagrams, still no interaction with the participants, nothing to capture their attention.

These mistakes – and many others it would come equally naturally to you to avoid – derive from an ignorance of people; of what inspires us and what alienates us; of what interests us and what sends us to sleep; of how we learn and how we react to being taught.

Let us rewrite the scenario, using all our conscious and unconscious understanding of people.

The 12 participants entered through the open double doors, paused to look round the square room with three round tables each with four chairs, and then sat down, chatting, in pairs and groups. In front of each chair was a pad of paper, a couple of pens, and a glass; bottles of mineral water stood in the centre of each table. Two large sliding windows were slightly open, and the scent of roses from an old rambler outside was just discernible.

The trainer was moving round the room, chatting to people as they came in. At 9.00am, when the course was due to start, she walked to the front of the room and smiled round at the people in the room. They stopped chatting, and looked at her expectantly.

She began: 'As you know, we're here to discuss and explore how management practices in your organisation need to adapt and evolve in response to some turbulent change that you are leading the organisation through. I've met most of you in the pre-course interviews, and we'll be investigating some of the topics and live management issues you raised.

But before we start, let's introduce ourselves and summarise for the rest of the group what we hope to get out of the next two days. Can we start with you, Jackie?'

And so on.

You will recognise this scenario as standard good training practice, certainly not training 'rocket science'. Yet even in this straightforward scenario, psychological principles have influenced the design of the training at well over a dozen points. From the number of participants to the style of the trainer's speech, from the fresh air in the room to the arrangement of the chairs, psychology has dictated good practice.

So it is clear that psychology is extremely relevant to training.

But chemistry is relevant to cookery, in much the same way. Yet chefs don't study chemistry. So why would trainers want to know about psychology? Before we answer this question, let us just be clear about what kind of knowledge of psychology this book is concerned with.

The scope of this book

Just before sitting down to start writing today, I was listening to Melvyn Bragg's 'Start the Week' on Radio 4. He had as his guests a number of scientists at the forefront of thinking in their fields, and he asked the biologist: 'What are the most interesting issues being addressed today in the field of biology?' The biologist replied: 'There are now two unexplained mysteries in biology. The first concerns the origin of life, and the second concerns how the human mind works.'

This comment seems to me to put this book in its appropriate context. The book is called 'Psychology for Trainers'. And among the many definitions of 'psychology', one that is often used is 'the science of the human mind'. Yet how the human mind works is still, today, a great unexplained mystery. So how can we use a science still in its infancy to inform a very practical and immediate application such as training?

The answer to that is 'very carefully'. There are relatively few cast-iron facts to be found in psychology. And the facts that there are cannot be applied in a general way: the human mind is so complex and human behaviour so varied, so responsive to slight changes in circumstance and meaning, that although psychologists may regard the great immutable laws of physics with envy, we certainly for now – and perhaps for ever – have to accept that psychology is unlikely to generate laws of similar stature and simplicity. This means that in applying lessons learned from psychology we must always resist the temptation to be dogmatic. In applying the lessons, we should be sure to remain open to discovering ways in which they *do not* apply.

Applying psychology to training is not like applying the principles of aerodynamics to aeroplane design. It is more like using a schoolboy knowledge of Latin to begin a relationship with an Italian lover; much better than nothing, but of necessity basic, tentative, experimental, and open to constant modification and learning.

You might be thinking by now that it would be better for trainers to leave psychology alone until it had matured a bit more, and work out what to do from their own and others' training experience alone. Yet that is not the thesis of this book, and it is not what I believe. First, the theory and practice of training has already been greatly influenced by psychology. (Your amused incredulity at the picture of 'training without psychology' with which this book opens is evidence of that.) So it is as well for trainers to understand those influences and to gain more control over them.

Second, if lessons learned from psychology are applied carefully, they are an immense resource for ideas in training. Third, trainers can benefit hugely from developing the capability for what I call a 'psychological frame of mind'. That is not to say this is the only, nor always the most appropriate, frame of mind for the trainer, but it is a very resourceful and creative state for her to have access to.

Let us look a little more closely at what I mean by a 'psychological frame of mind'.

The psychological frame of mind

Let me admit that for many people on training courses, the idea that their tutor might be possessed of a psychological frame of mind is not particularly appealing. In fact, some people would find it positively unnerving.

They associate the word 'psychological' with lying on a couch hearing their inner thoughts being interpreted by a mysterious, omniscient and controlling outsider. Or with 'psychiatry', the implication being that they are dysfunctional in some important way and the trainer will root out their problem – no matter how carefully they have hidden it until now – and force-feed them the appropriate medicine.

But this is not at all what I mean by a 'psychological frame of mind'. I mean nothing more nor less than a frame of mind that is:

■ focused on people, rather than on data or tasks

■ curious and exploratory rather than quick to draw conclusions

■ at least as ready to learn as to teach.

Why am I connecting these attitudes to psychology, when many would say they are simply general basic tenets of good training? I am doing so because I believe that a study of psychology does a great deal to foster and develop them, and does so in the following ways.

The focus on people, rather than data or tasks, is obviously encouraged by the study of psychology. Many definitions of psychology exist, but they all have the word 'human' in there somewhere:

■ 'the science of human behaviour'

■ 'the study of the human mind'

■ 'understanding what makes human beings tick'.

A curious and exploratory attitude results from studying a subject with hardly any absolutes – and that describes psychology exactly. Ask a psychologist a question about how people behave, and she will probably reply, 'It depends…' 'How much information can people assimilate at one go?' 'It depends.' 'What size of group can a single trainer manage?' 'It depends.' You might argue that a practical endeavour like training is better off without such equivocal expertise, without a school of thinking that raises more questions than it answers and increases rather than reduces the perceived complexity of the training task.

But the very absence of absolutes in the so-called science of human behaviour gives rise to a profound respect for people's complexity. With the psychological frame of mind, the trainer enters every training scenario prepared to be surprised. She approaches each group with the intent to find out about them rather than with the assumption that she already knows. (Every trainer can tell 'war stories' that demonstrate the complexity and unpredictability of individuals and groups. One of my favourites was when I used, for the 54th time, a teambuilding exercise requiring team members to build an apparatus to rescue a falling egg. The first 53 times I had used it, it had worked well. So I was approaching a dangerously complacent state of mind... rather than a psychological one. On this 54th occasion, the group rejected the exercise as sexist, as favouring the men in the team over the women. I immediately became considerably less complacent!)

Finally, readiness to learn is encouraged as a consequence of the 'youth' of psychology as a discipline. In such a young discipline, things yet to be investigated far outweigh things already understood. For every established 'fact' about the way people behave, there are hundreds of questions still to be answered. Indeed, every new finding simply raises further questions. Here is just one of an infinite number of possible examples: 'There is evidence of a link between schizophrenia and a biochemical disturbance affecting the central nervous system.' But what precisely is the nature of this link? How solid is the evidence? If there really is a link, which way round does it work? Does disturbed biochemistry lead to schizophrenia, or does schizophrenia lead to disturbed biochemistry? Why can the link be found in some schizophrenics, but not in all?

You can readily see how a psychological frame of mind leads a trainer to establish a learning partnership with those on her courses: she may offer the first input, but the questions and suggestions her participants raise will be as important as the input itself.

So in this book I try first and foremost to make the benefits of a psychological frame of mind easily accessible to fellow trainers. I do it by exploring those aspects of psychology most relevant to our work as trainers. I do it by giving alternative psychological approaches to some of our most burning questions. And I do it by acknowledging throughout that psychology cannot give us a recipe for success – but it can be both a supermarket where we can buy many of the ingredients and a training ground where we can learn how to cook with them.

In brief

So why would trainers want to know about psychology? Let's summarise the reasons:

▌ to understand how psychology has already influenced training practices, so that we as trainers can exercise more control and creativity

▌ to get new ideas and approaches that we can use to improve our effectiveness as trainers

▌ to develop a 'psychological frame of mind' – people-centred, curious and exploratory, always keen to learn.

2

Building Rapport, Establishing Credibility

When it works

Every trainer knows when she has rapport and credibility with a group. She can feel it. The specific feeling is probably different for each one of us, but a moment's reflection will remind you of what it is for you. Here is my own personal checklist – the private signals that tell me I am OK with the group, they are OK with me, and we can proceed.

- I feel interested in the group, curious about their preoccupations, hopes, and fears.
- I feel energetic.
- I feel like smiling, and humour comes easily.

One trainer I know, and sometimes work with, also experiences the last two 'rapport signals' when things are going well. In his case, the level of energy and creative humour which is sparked off is so high that he becomes amazingly entertaining: one participant on a course we ran together referred to his style affectionately as similar to that of a TV game show host!

When it is not working

The personal signals we get when we have failed to establish rapport and credibility with a group are even more recognisable – and potentially even more overpowering. The 'game show host' trainer I just referred to feels lethargy and irritability. This is how I feel when it is not working.

- I feel self-conscious.
- Often, my stomach feels uncomfortable.
- I feel tired in anticipation of the effort I must now put in to get the situation right.
- Sometimes I feel impatient with the group.
- I feel as if there is a fog between me and the group, as if we do not see and hear each other clearly; communication is an effort.

Uncomfortable as these feelings are, they are vital to our effectiveness as trainers. They are vital for two reasons. First, they tell us that the group is not ready to embark on the training agenda. The moment we become immune to these feelings, at that moment we become less sensitive and responsive to the group. And we may drop in and out of rapport with our participants at any stage of the programme, not just at the beginning: we need to know when we do so.

The second reason why these feelings are so important is that they give us the signal for becoming more resourceful when training gets difficult. We will discuss this in more depth in Chapter 7 on 'handling conflict'.

For now, let us take a step back and summarise the questions about rapport and credibility to which we trainers would particularly like some answers from psychology.

The issues for us as trainers

Building rapport and credibility is probably the aspect of our training practice that has the greatest impact on our effectiveness, and on our enjoyment of the training role. 'Rapport', 'credibility': such abstract concepts, with the most tangible of effects. Training can be a delight, almost a self-indulgence, certainly as heady as any of the performing arts; and it can be gut-wrenchingly, palm-prickingly, throat-parchingly grim. Rapport and credibility make the difference, for us as well as our participants.

Here are the questions we agonise over:

■ How can I build rapport quickly?

■ How can I establish the kind of credibility I need for people to learn from me without competing with them?

■ Why do I find it so easy to work with some people, so difficult with others?

■ What can I do if I take a dislike to one of my participants or he or she takes a dislike to me?

■ Why are some trainers so good at creating a relaxed atmosphere, so quick to win the respect and interest of a group, while others struggle?

■ How can I become excellent at building rapport and establishing credibility?

Insights from neurolinguistic programming (NLP)

Box 1 introduces neurolinguistic programming. It is relevant to the training issues we are discussing here because one of its central concepts is that of 'rapport', defined in NLP terms as 'a relationship of trust and responsiveness'. The NLP use of the term 'rapport', which is not about superficial liking but something rather deeper, also covers the issue of 'credibility'. If we have rapport, in the NLP sense, with people, they will think we are worth attending to. (As we will think they are.)

So let us explore what NLP tells us about rapport, and what we as trainers can learn from it.

First things first: build rapport with yourself

You might think only a split personality could have trouble building rapport with himself. In one way, this is true. For much psychological thinking maintains that we are all split personalities. Think of common expressions, such as 'I want to, but I don't think I should' or 'part of me wants to say 'yes', but part of me wants to say 'no''. Such expressions, and the experiences that give rise to them, are evidence that we do not function as completely integrated, unitary personalities: we have a number of subpersonalities, or 'parts'. Where these parts are in conflict, we do not have rapport with ourselves. (For other thinking along these lines, you might like to refer to the sections on transactional analysis in Chapter 7, pages 122–128.)

Box 1

INTRODUCTION TO NEUROLINGUISTIC PROGRAMMING (NLP)

▌ NLP began in the early 1970s when Richard Bandler, a student of psychology at the University of California, began working with John Grinder, then Assistant Professor of Linguistics. They wanted to discover what made people excellent communicators; so they studied three:

Fritz Perls, the innovative psychologist and originator of Gestalt therapy
Virginia Satir, the famous family therapist
Milton Erickson, the famous hypnotherapist.

▌ NLP now encompasses ways of thinking, tools and techniques that are not just about excellence in communication, but about excellence *per se*. It conveys a vision of a world where everyone can be outstanding. It is used by people in all walks of life, including sales, counselling, negotiation, leadership positions, and so on. It is also used by individuals who simply want to increase their own personal effectiveness and/or enjoyment of life.

▌ NLP is sometimes referred to as 'the psychology of excellence'.

Let me illustrate the above point with an example from a training situation. Suppose you were asked to deliver a workshop to help managers 'counsel staff out' in the most effective and humane way possible. And suppose in addition that you knew that redundancies had been decided on a last-in, first-out basis; that many poor performers were keeping their jobs; and that many good performers were losing theirs. Suppose you knew that some of the participants on your course were poor performers; and, finally, suppose you strongly disapproved of the whole redundancy programme.

You would not be in rapport with yourself running that workshop. One part of you would be wanting to do a good job. Another part of you would be wishing you did not have to. And yet another part of you would be resisting helping a poor performer learn skills to enable him to perpetrate what you saw as an injustice.

The thinking and research behind NLP suggest that when you are not in rapport with yourself, you will find it very hard to build rapport with other people. They will pick up mixed messages (your words at odds with your non-verbal behaviour, for example), and they will be at best confused, at worst mistrustful. They will not know where you are coming from, because in fact you will be coming from more than one place.

NLP provides us with a useful model for checking our level of rapport with ourselves. (See Table 1.)

What Table 1 implies for us as trainers is that we need to be able to say the following if we are going to deliver a programme effectively:

(Environment)	∎	'I'm glad to be delivering this programme *here*.'
(Behaviour)	∎	'I *shall be delivering* this programme.'
(Capability)	∎	'I *can* deliver this programme well.'
(Identity)	∎	'I'm *the right person* to deliver this programme.'
(Spirituality)	∎	'Delivering this programme *makes sense and has value*.'

LOGICAL LEVELS

We operate on many levels simultaneously. We are at our most effective at building relationships when, in relation to the specific issues important in the relationship, all these levels are in harmony.

Logical levels

Environment	➤ where and when; the context
Behaviour	➤ what we do
Capability	➤ our skill; how we do things
Belief	➤ what is important to us
Identity	➤ who we think we are
Spirituality	➤ what we think our place is in the greater scheme of things

So if we want to make an effective proposal of marriage, for example, we should:

- make it in a place where we have happy associations with our partner
- ask!
- ask lovingly!
- be sure we want to marry this person
- see this person as the right kind of partner for us
- see marriage to him or her as life-enhancing and as fulfilling our human potential.

If all these conditions are satisfied, he or she will find it hard to say no!

If we have trouble making any of the statements confidently about a programme we are about to deliver, we need to do some work to put it right before we enter the training room. In my redundancy counselling example above, the most urgent issues to be addressed are related to conflicts between 'behaviour' and 'belief'.

Building rapport with others

There are two particularly important ideas in NLP when it comes to building rapport with others. These are the ideas of 'pacing' and 'leading'. 'Pacing' is about meeting other people in their 'map of the world'. It is as if you were trying to get on a moving train: you stand a much better chance if you run at the same speed as the train, pacing it, before you jump. Once your speed is matched, you may meet.

So it is when we meet other people. They are moving at speed through a psychological terrain defined by themselves. We need to get on to that map, walking alongside them, before they can hear us.

On page 16 are two examples of dialogue between trainer and participant. In the first, the trainer fails to pace the participant. The trainer is talking about behaviour and skills; the participant is concerned about identity (see earlier text on logical levels). Rapport is broken by the third line in the exchange. In the second example, by contrast, the trainer gets alongside the participant's preoccupations immediately.

You can pace logical levels, body language, tone of voice, the metaphors and other imagery people use... you can pace anything about people's maps of the world. But the most important thing about pacing is that it gets you into the habit of attending closely to how the other person sees things. And that is at the heart of building rapport.

Once you have been accepted into the other person's map of the world (which you will feel, as the atmosphere between you becomes easy and relaxed), you have the opportunity to 'lead'. That means introducing new information or a new way of looking at things – the essence of the trainer's task.

First example of dialogue: no pacing

Trainer: Who has had some experience of giving presentations?

Participant: Presentations are only given by senior managers in this company.

Trainer: Can you tell me about a presentation outside the work environment that you've given?

Participant: I'm not the kind of person who pushes herself forward.

Trainer: So which skill would you like to focus on over the next three days?

Participant: I'm not even sure why I'm on this course.

Trainer: I'm sure you'll learn something useful, even if you don't give that many presentations.

Second example of dialogue: effective pacing

Trainer: Who has had some experience of giving presentations?

Participant: Presentations are only given by senior managers in this company.

Trainer: Who would count as 'senior managers'?

Participant: Not me, that's for sure.

Trainer: So tell me something about your role, and why you're on this course.

Participant: I was sent on the course by my manager. I'm a technical specialist, and have no intention of going into generalist management.

Trainer: Can you tell me some more about the technical work you do, so that I can think about which parts of this course might be useful to you?

One last word of warning: pacing is not about mimicry. Mimicry is copying some superficial aspect of other people's behaviour, without any real interest in what it tells us about how they see things. Mimicry breaks rapport, because the mimic is not in rapport with herself: her behaviour says, 'I'm attending to you'; her belief is, 'If I pretend to attend to you, you'll attend to me.'

A practical example of effective pacing and leading

I recently designed, with a skilled and experienced NLP practitioner, a director-level development programme for a large firm of lawyers. We knew that effective pacing was going to be vital, since these senior lawyers were dubious that training could offer them anything, and suspicious of notions of personal development. Their map of the world included terrain that many readers will instantly recognise – areas of belief such as these:

∎ You need training and development only if you are doing something wrong.

∎ At our stage, we are not doing anything wrong: we are successful so by definition we are effective; and if we are ineffective in any way, we need to hide it to maintain our organisational status and our self-respect.

∎ The route to advancement is via knowing the right people, not via increasing personal effectiveness in the job.

∎ No one except a lawyer in our firm can have anything useful to say to us about any of this: these two trainers are unlikely to appreciate the realities and the complexities of our professional lives.

We needed to get on to this map (pacing) and answer their reservations about the programme (leading).

Here are three of the ways we did it.

∎ We included in the tutor team an experienced and senior human resources director from their own firm:

he was a respected individual, who had spent a great deal of time talking one-to-one with senior lawyers about personal and development issues. He was, if you like, an easily recognisable 'landmark' from the participants' map of the world (pacing).

■ We stipulated that attendance on the programme would be voluntary: no nominations from others, however senior or influential, would be accepted. This showed that we understood participants' concern about attendance meaning failure (pacing) and were inviting them to understand this programme differently (leading).

■ Throughout the pre-programme literature, and in the course material itself, we used the vocabulary and concepts of the firm's own strategic initiative on 'differentiation'. We referred to 'differentiating learning', 'differentiating relationships', and 'differentiating communication', for example. We showed in this way that we understood and accepted the participants' priorities (pacing), while inviting them to consider how these priorities affected new areas, the areas of personal and professional development (leading).

These examples are just three of many: the key to pacing and leading effectively is to design and deliver every aspect of the training with these two questions uppermost in our minds:

■ What meanings will the participants attach to this? (pacing)

■ How can we make sure the meanings they attach are those most productive and developmental for them? (leading)

Insights from personality theory

In the pages above we have been examining some of the approaches NLP offers us for building rapport and establishing credibility with *anyone*. But we know that however effective we may become at doing this, it will always be easier with some people than with others. And the people I find it easiest to build rapport with may well be quite different from the people you find it easiest to build rapport with. We tend to get on with, and communicate most easily and effectively with, people who are more like us; it takes more effort with people who are very different. As trainers, we need some ways of identifying and thinking about the similarities and differences between people so that we can make good use of 'natural' rapport, and pay particular attention to building rapport when it does not come naturally.

Personality theory is the area of psychology that focuses on the abiding similarities and differences in behaviour, preference, and motivation between individual human beings. Of course, interest in these similarities and differences is many centuries older than psychology. The ancient Greeks identified four basic 'humours' underpinning individual characters; astrology attributes similarities and differences to the positions of planets when each of us was born. Unlike other schemata for understanding individual differences, however, personality theory rests on systematic objective research into how people behave, and that is why we as trainers should investigate the insights that it gives us.

In the following pages we shall look at a number of different theories about personality. Each has the potential to offer the trainer new ways of understanding similarities and differences between herself and the group, and between individuals in the group. Each has the potential to give the trainer ideas on how to build rapport and establish credibility with different 'types' of people.

It is also important to look at more than one way of understanding personality. Many psychologists have tried, and are still trying, to produce the definitive description, and some may claim that they have done so. But we as trainers will benefit most if we view all the approaches as containing some usable and useful elements, but none as containing the whole truth.

Before we look at the variety, however, let us look at one specific theory in depth. I have chosen it because it is fairly simple, it is particularly relevant to situations where people are learning, and it encourages us to look at people who are different from ourselves with interest, rather than with judgement.

Jung's theory focuses on the cognitive aspects of personality – that is, how we think, how we gather information about the world and use that information to make decisions. It is these aspects of personality that play a major part in influencing our style of communication – both how we most naturally and effectively receive information and how we most naturally and effectively transmit it. These aspects also have a profound influence on how we learn (see also Chapter 7 on 'Mixed Personality Classes' in my last book, *Designing Training* (IPD, 1996)). So it is to these aspects that we as trainers need to pay particular attention.

Jung's four dimensions of thinking

Jung based his theory on observations that he made over years of clinical practice, talking with his 'patients', listening carefully to the different ways in which they thought about their worlds. Since his original formulation the theory has acquired added credibility through the research into and development of a questionnaire designed to establish the Jungian 'type' of anyone who completed it: the Myers-Briggs Type Indicator (MBTI*).

The four dimensions of difference that Jung identified are these:

* Copyright Oxford Psychologists Press

1 Extraverted thinking versus *introverted thinking*

> Extraverted thinkers derive most of their energy and information for thinking from contact with the outside world, of people, events, and actions. Introverted thinkers, on the other hand, derive most of their energy and information from their own inner world of ideas and impressions. Extraverts tend to think actively, trying things out, 'thinking aloud'. Introverts tend to think reflectively, and need time and space to do so.

2 Sensing thinking versus *intuitive thinking*

> Sensing thinkers pay most attention to the evidence of their senses: what they can see, hear and touch. They are pragmatic, need proof, and are often suspicious of theory. Intuitive thinkers, on the other hand, are more interested in possibility than fact. They like to think conceptually, value ideas, and are easily bored by practical data.

3 Thinking thinking versus *feeling thinking*

> Thinking thinkers decide on the basis of objective logic and analysis. They are detached at the point of drawing their conclusions, although they may well consider more subjective aspects, such as feelings and values, at a later point. Feeling thinkers make decisions in a way that integrates fact and feeling, and can sometimes place the emphasis on feeling over fact. Values – their own and/or other people's – are an inseparable part of the equation for feeling thinkers. If a decision does not feel right, they probably will not make it.

4 Judging thinking versus *perceiving thinking*

> Judging thinkers like closure, so they can move on to the next thing. They tend to be decisive and to live life in an organised and planned way. They do not much like being caught unawares. Perceiving thinkers like to go with the flow, leave things open for as long as possible to see what new angles present themselves. They tend to think and

live life spontaneously, quick on their feet but often ill-prepared. They enjoy surprising turns of events, which they see as challenging and interesting, rather than threatening.

Jung suggests that each of us has a preference for one of each pair of thinking styles. These preferences are deep-rooted and determine what comes naturally to us, at what we are most readily effective. I, for example, am an extraverted intuitive thinking perceiving thinker. Enthusiasm for identifying and trying out new ideas comes naturally to me, and I can adapt easily to unpredictable situations. On the other hand, long periods of careful planning and meticulous organising wear me out, and I have had to work hard to develop a reasonable competence in project management.

Insights from Jung's theory for us as trainers

You may already have been thinking, as you read through the descriptions of the different preferences above, thoughts along the lines of 'So that's why I can never get my point across to so-and-so! He's only interested in ideas; I keep giving him the facts!' One of the most useful aspects of Jung's theory is that it is often possible to guess what preferences people have – we all give away our preferences every time we speak:

∎ by the amount of 'airtime' we use, and by how publicly we do our thinking (extraverts use lots of airtime and do lots of public thinking)

∎ by the words we use and the stories we tell (sensing thinkers are good at providing detail and examples)

∎ by the level of detachment with which we debate things (thinking thinkers can be pretty tough when they are arguing a point, and take no prisoners!)

∎ by the degree of organisation versus spontaneity in our communication (perceiving thinkers love to play with words and ideas).

And so on, and so on. This means that when we want to build rapport with someone, we can use Jung's framework of differences to communicate with them in the ways they will find most engaging.

Also, when rapport seems hard to build, we can look for reasons in Jung's theory, rather than simply blame ourselves and get despondent. I well remember a training experience I had with a group of 20 engineers on a teamworking skills course. For a whole morning I laboured, in the absence of any feedback from the group, trying to make the ideas and exercises I was putting across ever more entertaining and stimulating. The group was incredibly quiet – without even the usual 'noisy' or 'difficult' participant to get things going. At lunch-time I confided in my client – 'I don't think the group like me: I'm not getting anything back from them'. I was at my wits' end. After lunch, we scored the participants on the Myers-Briggs Type Indicator (the questionnaire that establishes thinking preferences). We discovered that every single participant was an introverted thinker. They were quiet because they were thinking. My anxiety immediately diminished, I stopped my frenetic attempts to entertain, slowed the pace and gave people more time to think. By the end of the afternoon, both I and the participants were communicating in a relaxed, reflective way, much more appropriate to their thinking preferences.

Finally, as trainers we need to know ourselves so that we know when we will be effective acting naturally, and when we have to adapt our natural style. Jung's theory is a good one to apply to ourselves: it highlights some personal characteristics very relevant to training, and it does so in a way that helps us develop. If you want more help in working out which your preferences are, you can use the short questionnaire in Chapter 4 of *Working in Teams* (London, IPD, 1995), an earlier book of mine which explores Jung's theory in relation to team effectiveness. The questionnaire is reproduced below.

Action

I enjoy meetings. ❏

I like to talk my ideas through with someone. ❏

I find I get energy and ideas from lots of discussion. ❏

I'm often one of the main contributors in a discussion. ❏

Other people usually know what I'm thinking. ❏

Interruptions and changes of tack don't bother me. ❏

I'm often the first to state my opinion. ❏

Sometimes I worry that I've talked too much in a meeting. ❏

I like to get other people's ideas and reactions to my ideas. ❏

I think it's pointless to spend lots of time thinking without doing anything. ❏

Reflection

I like to reflect thoroughly on an issue before saying what I think. ❏

I'm often quiet at meetings. ❏

Sometimes I get exhausted by having to explain things to people and listen to their views. ❏

I tend to involve people in things I'm working on after I've done some thinking of my own. ❏

People quite often ask me how I came to my conclusions. ❏

I think it's all too easy to rush into action without thinking things through. ❏

I'm often the last to comment on an issue. ❏

I sometimes feel people underestimate the amount of thought I've put into a decision. ❏

I sometimes neglect to consult people. ❏

I like to think what I say is well thought through. ❏

Facts

I'm known for taking a pragmatic approach. ❏

I often remind people of the realities of a situation. ❏

I sometimes get impatient with airy-fairy ideas. ❏

Ideas

I'm known as an ideas person. ❏

I prefer to think about the big picture rather than about the details. ❏

People often comment on my enthusiasm. ❏

Facts (*continued*)

I think people often pay too little attention to the facts. ❏

I'm often the one in a meeting who reminds others of important points of detail. ❏

I get people to make the steps in their logic explicit. ❏

I like to follow an argument through to the end to check it will work. ❏

I believe it's important to look at precedents and previous approaches which have worked. ❏

I think you can learn a lot from the past. ❏

I am more convinced by facts and logic than by inspirational talk. ❏

Ideas (*continued*)

I am good at creating patterns and links out of situations and facts. ❏

I enjoy ideas and concepts. ❏

I believe it's often useful to forget all about the constraints and think 'blue sky'. ❏

I get frustrated by people who need everything spelt out. ❏

I often think of new possibilities. ❏

I'm sometimes caught out by matters of fact and detail. ❏

I get bored with analysing the past and the present. ❏

I think opportunities for positive change are often lost because of pessimists and nit-pickers. ❏

Logic

I can be very detached when it comes to making decisions. ❏

People would say I was a logical thinker. ❏

Sometimes I hurt people unintentionally when I'm simply trying to get to the right answer. ❏

I believe discussion, debate and challenges are necessary to test ideas and proposals. ❏

I think it's more important to make a sound decision than to take people with you. ❏

Values

I naturally think of the human aspects of issues. ❏

I think heart and soul are just as important as logic. ❏

My own value system often influences my approach to problems. ❏

I feel uncomfortable when there is conflict and disharmony in groups to which I belong. ❏

I think the important thing in decision-making is to win people's commitment. ❏

(continued overleaf)

Logic (*continued*)

When I'm under pressure,
I put the job first and can be
tough with the people. ❑

I think emotions get in the way
of good decision-making. ❑

I don't generally allow my own
values and personal feelings to
influence decisions. ❑

I think the primary justification
for doing something must lie
in logical analysis of the
pros and cons. ❑

I would say the more pressure
I'm under, the more rational
I become. ❑

Values (*continued*)

I believe getting people's trust
is as important as being right. ❑

I am sensitive to other people's
values and feelings. ❑

When I am under pressure,
a sense of harmony and
belonging become even more
important to me. ❑

I am good at building rapport
with people, without really trying. ❑

I consider mercy to be more
essential than justice. ❑

Order

I'm often the one who organises
agendas for meetings. ❑

I'm known for my good
timekeeping. ❑

I think it's important to plan
ahead, and keep to the plan
unless you make explicit provision
for change. ❑

I get impatient with indecisive
meetings. ❑

I make sure people are clear
about who is to do what by when. ❑

I like advance notice so I can
prepare properly. ❑

I think it's often more important
just to make a decision than to
make 'the right' decision. ❑

Spontaneity

I don't mind thinking on my feet –
in fact, I quite enjoy it. ❑

I think it's important to keep an
open mind for as long as possible. ❑

Sometimes I get so caught up in
the discussion that I forget what
we're meant to be deciding. ❑

I think a lot of problems are
caused by over-decisiveness. ❑

Sometimes I feel as if I've been
rushed into making my mind up. ❑

I am very responsive to new
demands and new information. ❑

I get bored by predictability. ❑

Order (continued)		Spontaneity (continued)	
I am often the one who tries to move discussion forward to a conclusion.	❏	Sometimes I procrastinate, out of a sense that something may turn up which changes the whole picture.	❏
I work in a structured, methodical way.	❏	I enjoy the process of getting to a decision more than making the decision itself.	❏
Sometimes when I've made my mind up I refuse to enter any more debate on an issue.	❏	I am good at doing things at the last minute.	❏

Let us now move on from examining in depth how Jung's theory can enlighten our approach to building rapport. Let us consider some of the variety of personality theories so that we can extend even further our ability to communicate flexibly, understand difference creatively and constructively, and know ourselves better.

Vive la différence: *some more theories of personality*

Not only do psychologists differ in the way they 'slice up' personality, in the dimensions they consider to be important dimensions of difference; they differ even in how they *define* personality. Freud defined personality as the unconscious hidden and unknown basis of everything we do. Allport – one of the earliest personality theorists – defined it as 'the dynamic organisation within an individual of those psychophysical systems that determine his characteristic behaviour and thought'. Skinner, the famous behaviourist (whose work we look at in more depth in Chapter 8), considered that personality does not exist: it is simply something psychologists like to talk about! Skinner's view is that all that matters is our behaviour, and we do not need to talk or think in terms of traits or dimensions underlying that behaviour.

There are some fundamental differences in the way psychologists have formulated personality theories that are of particular significance in the training context. Table 2 opposite identifies these, and encourages you to decide which psychological position matches your own fundamental beliefs about people. You will easily see the implications of the different positions for training, and the effects that being at one or other end of each spectrum will have on the trainer's approach. You will also see that these fundamental beliefs will influence profoundly who you naturally build rapport with in the training context. For example, if you believe people have a high level of control over their behaviour but one of your participants believes the converse, the way you talk about personal development and change will probably be incomprehensible or even offensive to her. To communicate effectively with her, you will need to avoid emphasising her personal opportunities to behave differently, and instead emphasise the interaction between her and her environment, identifying where the environment is helpful to her and where it is not. Perhaps understanding the difference in your philosophies, and recognising that both philosophies are valid, will help you not to feel irritated when she claims 'I can't help reacting to my boss like that; that's the way things are in our organisation.'

When you have determined where you stand on each of these major assumptions, a comparison of your positions can help you assess the importance of these assumptions to your own understanding of personality. Those assumptions that you feel very strongly about and have marked with a 1 or a 5 probably play a very important role in your personal philosophy.

You should note that there are no correct answers to the questions. Different personality theorists vary markedly in their position on each of these assumptions. Each adopts the position that appears most commendable or compelling.

Table 2

EXAMINING PHILOSOPHICAL ASSUMPTIONS

Each philosophical assumption is presented in this table as a bipolar dimension along which a person's view can be placed according to the degree to which he or she agrees with one or the other extreme. You can rate your own views on a scale from 1 to 5. For each assumption, if you completely agree with the first statement, rate the issue as number 1. If you completely agree with the second statement, rate the issue as number 5. If you agree only moderately with either statement, number 2 or 4 would best reflect your view. If you are neutral toward the assumption, or believe that the best position is a synthesis of the two extremes, rate it as number 3.

1_____   2_____   3_____   4_____   5_____

freedom   determinism

People basically have control over their own behaviour and understand the motives behind their behaviour.

The behaviour of people is basically determined by internal or external forces over which they have little, if any, control.

1_____   2_____   3_____   4_____   5_____

constitutional   situational

Inherited and inborn characteristics have the most important influence on a person's behaviour.

Factors in the environment have the most important influence on a person's behaviour.

1_____   2_____   3_____   4_____   5_____

uniqueness   universality

Each individual is unique and cannot be compared with others.

People are basically very similar in nature.

1_____   2_____   3_____   4_____   5_____

proactive   reactive

Human beings primarily act on their own initiative.

Human beings primarily react to stimuli from the outside world.

1_____   2_____   3_____   4_____   5_____

optimistic   pessimistic

Significant changes in personality and behaviour can occur throughout the course of a lifetime.

A person's personality and behaviour are essentially stable and unchanging.

Adapted from Engler (1985)

A 'complete' model of personality

Before we leave the issue of how different we all are, let us look at the longest-established detailed and complete (in the sense that it purports to cover all aspects of our personality) formulation of the dimensions of difference: Cattell's psychometric trait theory.

Cattell defined personality in 1950 as 'that which permits a prediction of what a person will do in a given situation'. For example, if in situations where hard work is required, one individual opens a book, puts his feet up and reads, while another rolls his sleeves up and applies himself, we might suggest a personality trait scale with 'diligence' at one end and 'laziness' at the other.

Cattell analysed 18,000 adjectives commonly used to describe people. He compared people's descriptions of themselves (in questionnaires) with other people's descriptions of them (in school records, job appraisals and so on). He also conducted what he called 'objective' tests, where descriptions and measurement of people were taken without those people knowing on what they were being described and measured.

Through his analysis, Cattell decided that there were basically 16 dimensions which between them captured all the important personality differences between people. He called these dimensions the 16 personality factors, and they are listed in Table 3.

The next time you find yourself experiencing a 'personality clash', you might like to think about the 16PF dimensions and try to identify on which dimension you are clashing. Doing that usually helps you find ways through the clash.

Training issues in psychometric testing

Before we leave the subject of personality questionnaires, we should pause to consider whether and when we should actually use these psychological instruments in the training context.

Table 3

CATTELL'S 16PF

■ The 16PF (= 16 Personality Factors) is a questionnaire designed to measure a person against Cattell's 16 basic temperament and ability traits.

■ The factors are currently:

A	Warmth	the extent to which you have a warm genuine interest in people, and seek close relationships
B	Reasoning ability	the number of reasoning items on the questionnaire you get right, in relation to the general population
C	Emotional stability	how calmly you deal with life's ups and downs; how steady your mood is
E	Dominance	how forceful you are in taking the lead and expressing your views
F	Liveliness	how lively, enthusiastic and spontaneous you are
G	Rule-consciousness	the extent to which you feel obliged to follow rules and regulations; dutifulness
H	Social boldness	how socially confident you are
I	Sensitivity	how much importance you attach to subjective judgements, and to the cultural side of life
L	Vigilance	how questioning you are of others' motives
M	Abstractedness	the extent to which you focus on the broader issues rather than fact and detail
N	Privateness	how likely you are to reveal information about yourself
O	Apprehension	how self-critical you are
Q1	Openness to change	the extent to which you seek purposeful change and new ideas
Q2	Self-reliance	the extent to which you need a sense of belonging
Q3	Perfectionism	the extent to which you have well-defined personal standards, and are disciplined in meeting them
Q4	Tension	the amount of physical energy you feel; the extent to which you are restless, driven

They are in fact used quite widely. The one that is most used is the Myers-Briggs Type Indicator, for a number of reasons. First, it is relevant to many different training agendas, including team development, and interpersonal and communication skills development of all kinds. Second, it is a well-researched 'respectable' instrument. Third, it is what I call a 'safe' psychometric: it does not reveal things about people that they will be uncomfortable to know, or have others know, and it encourages people to decide whether or not the profile that the questionnaire reveals is their 'true' profile. They remain in control.

These are important points for us as trainers to remember in deciding if and when to use personality questionnaires. On the plus side, people often find them fun, most people like finding out more about themselves, and they can add a deeper dimension to training (see also my comments on people's need for 'self-actualisation' in Chapter 4). On the minus side, some people are frightened or irritated by them, and they can introduce a spurious 'scientific' element into the training room.

On balance, I think it is permissible to use psychometric questionnaires provided that we adhere to the following principles:

▮ We should always ask participants' permission to administer tests, and make it perfectly possible for people to refuse.

▮ We should clarify exactly why we are proposing them, what they will tell us, and how we are planning to use them.

▮ We should make clear in advance where the information will go; for example, will it go to the individual alone, to the whole group, or to the organisation? (This last option is *not* recommended.)

▮ We should make sure individuals have the opportunity to receive some personal feedback on their profile, if they want it.

The other thing we have to remember as trainers is that psychometric questionnaires can be administered and interpreted only by people who have been appropriately trained and licensed. While you need not be a psychologist to use them, the training process is quite lengthy and expensive. Many training objectives can be better met by using more informal self-analysis quizzes, which have not been scientifically researched, or 360-degree feedback questionnaires. The less rigorous nature of these kinds of instruments makes it easier for participants to 'take or leave' the results – and that is often more appropriate.

In brief

■ The issues of building rapport and establishing credibility with the group are key for us as trainers. Probably more than anything else, they determine our effectiveness, and our enjoyment of what we do.

■ Two areas of psychology are of particular relevance to these issues: neurolinguistic programming ('the psychology of excellence' in communication and in relationships) and personality theory (the psychology of individual differences).

■ Neurolinguistic programming (NLP) suggests to us that we need to:

    ☐ ensure we are 'in rapport with' ourselves; that our identity, values, capability and behaviour are in tune with the job we are doing

    ☐ understand and engage with our participants' map of reality

    ☐ only then introduce new information and perspectives.

■ Personality theory suggests to us that we need to:

    ☐ remain open-minded and creative in understanding why individual participants respond to us in the different ways they do

☐ become aware of our own preferences and traits, so that we know when we need to adapt our natural style to meet the needs and engage the attention of our participants.

3 Getting Information Across

It is true that, in many kinds of training, getting information across is not the primary goal. Unlike education, training is more about involving people in processes than it is about transmitting data to them. When we run an appraisal skills workshop, for example, we could probably summarise the entire 'content' of a two-day programme on a single page of A4. The most important activities – and the ones that take by far the most time – are discussion between participants and role-plays of appraisals.

Yet we cannot afford to ignore the issue of getting information across. We have to be able to provide introductory information on a huge range of topics, information that engages and stimulates; we have to be able to give instructions for exercises so that our participants are clear about what they have to do; we have to be able to summarise information coming from them in a way they appreciate. Also, at times, we do have to get large amounts of information across, of many kinds: about research, about theories, about how to do things, about the organisation that participants belong to... Imagine an induction programme, for example, or a workshop to explore the implications of a proposed change in organisational structure.

So in this chapter we shall look at what psychology has to tell us about getting information across effectively. We shall focus in particular on research into perception, attention and short-term memory and also take a quick look at the world of neurophysiology.

Being trainers, we must not forget that getting information across is as much about the relationship between the information-giver and information-getter as it is about the way the information is structured. So we shall keep in mind the insights we gained in the last chapter on building rapport and establishing credibility – and we shall concentrate in this chapter on some of the 'hard' facts (ie, certain and quantified) that psychology has to offer on how information should be presented.

When it works

I was running a train-the-trainer programme recently which had probably the highest information content of any programme I have ever run. I knew I was getting it across when I saw people jotting things down thoughtfully and, best of all, when I heard them later in the programme using some of the theories and models that I had introduced them to.

When it is not working

But in the very same programme, I knew I was not getting the information across when I saw:

- constant head-down writing as I was talking (too much information, not being digested by the participants but simply recorded verbatim)
- people reading ahead in the workbook (too little information, or information not made relevant to them)
- puzzled faces (too much information, or unclear information)
- exhausted faces, people holding their heads, glazed eyes (information overload!)

And of course there is one of the worst training experiences I know: when you give participants a task (a question to discuss, a simulation to act out, a case study to explore) and they come back having done the 'wrong work'. Then you know with complete certainty that you did not get the information across, and that their time has been wasted – at least to some degree.

The issues for us as trainers

When we have experiences like the ones I have just described, we ask ourselves these questions:

- How much information can people take in at one go?
- What is the best way of structuring it?
- How can I organise things so that people can take in as much as possible?
- How much variability is there between people in terms of their capacity to process information?
- How can I become excellent at getting information across?

We can never get all the information across to all of the participants all of the time. But we can learn how to do it better, and we do. So let us reinforce and speed up our learning by looking at what psychology has to tell us.

Insights from the psychology of perception, attention, and short-term memory

Box 2 on page 39 introduces the idea of people as information-processing machines. For us as trainers this idea – dreamed up by psychologists as a useful device to structure their research into how people notice and remember things – is worth thinking about: it challenges us to find ways to avoid overloading the machine, or clogging it up, and to feed information into it in the way best suited to its manner of working.

The magic number seven

> *Question* 'How much information can a person take in at one go?'
>
> *Answer* 'Seven things, plus or minus two.'

It appears from a huge number and variety of experiments that most people can perceive about seven things simultaneously, can remember about seven things without their being repeated, and can 'take in' about seven things without a break or breathing space.

But before we all rush off and rewrite all our course notes so that everything is presented in units of seven things or fewer (which certainly is not a bad rule of thumb) let us delve a little deeper into what constitutes a 'thing'. Because that is where psychology really tells us something interesting.

The power of meaning

> *Question* 'How big is a 'thing'?'
>
> *Answer* 'It depends on what you mean by it.'

A thing can be a single letter or it can be thousands of letters... In a random sequence of letters of the alphabet, like PBAAIHQZB, a thing is a single letter, and we can 'take in' only seven of them at one time. In a sequence of familiar song lyrics, we can take in seven whole lyrics, and thus thousands of individual letters. Here are some more examples of 'things' of different sizes; all of them will count as only one thing in terms of determining how many of them we are able to take in.

- a digit   5
- a number that means
  something to us   1998
- a pronounceable nonsense syllable   JAX
- a phrase   MAN BITES
                                       DOG
- a shape   ▽

Box 2

THE HUMAN INFORMATION PROCESSOR

In the late 1950s and early 1960s, when the age of computing was dawning, psychologists decided that a useful metaphor for – or model of – the way the human mind works could be drawn from that infant world of computing. The diagram below illustrates a typical form of the model.

Information processing system

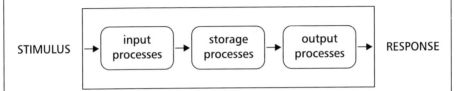

This way of looking at the human mind did indeed result in a number of important insights which in their turn provoked a great deal of subsequent investigation. (Because psychology is such a young science, which attempts to explain such complex and infinitely variable phenomena, often the most significant consequence of any new theory is the surge of experimental activity that arises to test the theory. The theory itself is usually fairly rapidly demonstrated to have serious limitations, but new insights come from the experiments.)

Some of the key insights resulting from the theory of the 'human information processor' were the following:

- The way the mind deals with incoming information can be viewed as a sequence of stages. Each stage can be investigated separately. The early, 'input', stages, are perception, attention, and short-term memory.
- The capacity of the human information processor, just like the capacity of technological information processors, is limited. The input processes must select information from a huge and potentially unmanageable bombardment.
- Attention is necessary to make the selection.

- a word   HOPELESS
- a name we know   John F Kennedy.

What determines the size of a thing is its meaning. A thing is a 'unit of meaning', if you like. So we can take in seven units of meaning at once.

Just to make it all even more complicated – and even more interesting – units of meaning are different for different individuals. So the sequence of numbers '200382' is a single 'thing' for me, because it is the date of my son's birth. For you, it might be two things ('200' and '382'), or six, or any number in between.

So where does all this leave us as trainers, trying to get information across?

- We should never *over*estimate the amount of *meaning* people can take in at one go (seven bits of meaning is not very many... I reckon when I do an introduction to the Myers-Briggs, which has four dimensions with two preferences on each dimension – see the previous chapter if you need a reminder on this – I am stretching people's information processing capabilities to their limit).

- We should never *under*estimate the amount of *data* people can take in, if it is meaningfully structured. Remember that we will all sit happily for an hour or more listening to a really good story that has meaning for us. But if we expect anyone to sit through an hour of bullet points on 'how to be an effective team leader', we deserve to have our training licence revoked immediately! The search to make the information we have for participants on our courses meaningful to them is infinitely more important than the search to parcel it up in digestible chunks.

- That having been said, quantity does matter. Research into short-term memory, perception and attention certainly supports our instinct to 'keep it simple', to alternate information-giving with activity, and to use all kinds of visual aids, notes, pictures and so on to reduce the load on memory wherever we can.

How long can people stay attentive?

Question 'How long can people stay attentive?'

Answer 'How long is a piece of string?'

Although as trainers we might hope that psychology can offer us the definitive answer to this question, so that we can make all our tutor inputs 10 minutes long in the confident knowledge that this is the average attention span of an adult, I am afraid that psychology has no such certainty to offer us. In fact it takes only a moment's reflection to realise it could not. We can attend without missing a beat to a gripping film three hours in length; yet our attention can fail us from the moment a person we have previously experienced to be boring opens his or her mouth to speak.

As was the case when we looked at how *much* we can attend to, so it is when we look at how *long* we can attend for: it all depends on meaning.

It is meaning that captures our attention, as well as meaning that sustains it. A simple example of this occurs in what psychologists call, somewhat pretentiously, the 'cocktail party phenomenon'. This 'phenomenon' happens when we are attending closely and apparently fully to a conversation, not noticing any of the other conversations going on around us, when suddenly someone somewhere else says our name – and our attention is immediately caught. Even though they may not be referring to us, but to a namesake, they have captured our attention – because our name is probably the single most meaning-loaded word in the whole of human language, for us.

Positioning information for maximum impact

Question 'How do I make sure the most important things I have to get across receive the most attention?'

Answer 'By putting them at the beginning, or at the end.'

Research into short-term memory identified two of the most consistent, most predictable features of the human information processor: the 'primacy effect' and the 'recency effect'. Figure 1 shows the results of a typical experiment, and also gives you a feel for the kind of detailed, painstaking, controlled research that psychologists have carried out in the field of memory.

Figure 1

RESEARCH INTO PRIMACY AND RECENCY EFFECTS

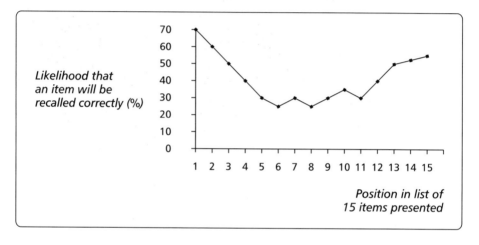

In this experiment, called a 'free-recall task', people are presented with sequences of 15 words. They are asked to recall as many of them as they can, soon after the sequence has been presented. They can recall them in any order they choose.

You can see from the graph that the probability that a word will be recalled depends on where in the sequence it was presented. If it was presented first, it is most likely to be recalled (primacy effect); if it was presented very near the beginning, it stands a better chance of being recalled than words in the middle of the sequence (primacy effect); if it was presented at or very near the end of the sequence, it is again more likely to be recalled (recency effect). The primacy effect is generally stronger and much longer-lasting than the recency effect.

Many other experimental tasks have demonstrated the primacy and recency effects, including:

- paired-associate learning (where people are given a list of pairs of words to learn and are tested by being given one word from a pair and asked to supply its 'partner')
- the 'probe task' (where people are asked to memorise a sequence of items and are tested by being given one of the items and asked to give the item that followed it).

Given the general absence of simple, clear and absolutely reliable facts psychology can give us on the hugely flexible human information processor, the primacy and recency effects really deserve our attention as trainers. How can we exploit them?

- Obviously, we can put the most important information at the beginning and end of information-giving sessions.
- We can avoid putting anything at the beginning that will 'switch people off': anything boring, or anything that will provoke a rejecting reaction. (I vividly remember an occasion when a senior manager began a presentation on a company reorganisation with a short statement of appreciation for the consultants who had helped him in his thinking: his audience glazed over instantly and visibly at the mention of the consultancy's name, since they were universally regarded by the workforce as manipulative and self-serving.)
- We can warn people when 'the end is nigh' – if we say, for example, 'there is just one more point to be made before we go into the discussion', then attention will peak again briefly.
- We can create as many primacy and recency effects as possible, by breaking up the information-giving component of any training. We do this instinctively, of course, but there is sound justification from

psychology for this practice. There has to be some 'middle' of course: you cannot just have a sequence of beginnings and ends. In fact, if you have too regular a pattern of short information-giving sessions the primacy and recency effects begin to apply to whole sessions (in other words, people attend to the first and last session of each day, but not the ones in between!); but you can certainly make a big deal of the beginnings and endings you have, and you can avoid long information-giving 'middles'.

∎ We can make absolutely sure that we never waste a 'beginning', the prime time for getting information across.

Getting people into their most information-receptive state of mind

> *Question* 'Do individuals vary from day to day, and from hour to hour, in terms of how much they can take in?'
>
> *Answer* 'You bet they do!'

As trainers we can increase our participants' total capacity for information. We can do it by:

∎ making the information meaningful to them (see earlier sections of this chapter)

∎ talking their language (see Chapter 2)

∎ demonstrating ourselves to be likeable and credible (see Chapter 2).

We can also do it by ensuring that their physical state of being is the best it can be for attending to and processing information.

Psychologists are very fond of studying people by pushing them to their extremes, to their limits, and seeing what happens. The cracks in our performance that show when we are operating at our limits give essential clues to how we work. During the Second World War, an extreme condition for testing people's attention processes came about naturally. And not only was it interesting for psychologists to study how people responded under that condition; it was also critical operationally. So the 'vigilance task' was born. Box 3 describes one of the classic types of experiment.

Box 3

A CLASSIC VIGILANCE STUDY

At Cambridge University in the 1940s, a group of psychologists designed a simulated cockpit, which became known as the 'Cambridge Cockpit'. People were required to sit in this cockpit and do work similar to that of a pilot on a long flight. They had to monitor a range of dials and gauges, and respond to a variety of signals. People's performance over many continuous hours of such work was studied, and a number of interesting 'cracks' in their perception and attention processes were demonstrated.

- Subjects became slower at responding to signals, or needed signals to be more noticeable before they responded.
- The pattern of errors tended to be that the correct responses were made, but too late. Incorrect responses at the right time were not so common.
- Subjects started to estimate time more and more inaccurately.
- Even that most vital of signals, the needle on the fuel gauge, was ignored when the subject was very fatigued. So some experiments ended abruptly, with the plane 'crashing'!

As psychologists investigated people's performance on vigilance tasks further, they discovered that the 'amount of attention' and the quality of attention processes available to people were not fixed, but could be raised and lowered in some fairly predictable ways. (A 'vigilance task' is a task that requires a person to pay attention actively, because the task is intrinsically boring and goes on for a long time.) The most important and well-established factors affecting people's capacity to pay attention seem to be the following:

- Lack of sleep: sleep loss impairs attention processes, and when it is extreme (100 hours and more of continuous wakefulness), delusions and hallucinations can occur; more typically, with smaller amounts of sleep deprivation, people either become slower, taking longer to perceive and respond, or, if they are forced to respond quickly, they make more mistakes.

- Drugs: a variety of drugs have an effect on people's perception and attention processes, and it is often for such an effect that people take 'recreational' (and illegal) drugs; but perhaps the finding most interesting and relevant to those of us who would prefer to stay on the right side of the law relates to caffeine (widely and legally available in tea, coffee and Coca Cola!); in brief, caffeine in moderate rather than extreme doses improves perception and attention.

- Motivation: even when people are so fatigued that their perception and attention processes are extremely slow and full of mistakes, their performance will be immediately improved by introducing a powerful new incentive or by changing the task to a more interesting one.

- Knowledge of results: knowledge of results improves perception and attention performance mainly because it motivates us, but even so it is worthy of special mention because it is very effective, and because it is relevant to training; in the 'Cambridge Cockpit', subjects maintained good performance for much longer if they were given periodic information on how well they were doing.

These findings tell us a lot about the conditions that we need to create as trainers to ensure our participants have the best chance to take information in.

Of course, you might be reading this section and saying to yourself: 'What could a course of mine possibly have in common with a 'vigilance task'? I go out of my way to make courses interesting, not boring; and the information

I present is nothing like signals on a radar screen!'

Let me challenge your thinking in two ways. First, for many of our participants, even the best training programme can sometimes feel a bit like a test of endurance. They are used to being active; we expect them to sit for long periods. They are used to deciding what they will do, and in what order; we ask them to follow our programme. They are used to a great variety of activity; we ask them to spend eight hours at a stretch on their development, and perhaps on one topic.

Second, even though the most exact research has been done in the extreme conditions of the vigilance task, there is plenty of evidence that the things found there to enhance and detract from attention are no different from the things that determine whether we stay awake during a concert, or remember the plot of a play.

Insights from neurophysiology

The central nervous system is the physical location of the human information processor (by 'central nervous system' I mean the brain, the spinal cord, and the nerve cells, or 'neurons', contained within them). So we might be tempted to think that if we can understand how the central nervous system works, what kind of information it registers most readily and most permanently, how much it can handle at a time, and so on, then we will understand how to get information across in the best possible way.

It seems, however, that the day when we achieve that precision of understanding of how the physical apparatus of our minds works is unimaginably far off. The sheer complexity of what we are trying to understand is baffling. There are billions of neurons in the central nervous system. They are connected to each other via many different pathways. Not only that, the connections between them change constantly, as we learn, as we mature, as we age. And even if there were a complete and accurate description of the physical workings of our information-processing system, we would not be able to comprehend the quantity of information in that description.

However, some of the basic and well-known features of our central nervous system are worth our thinking about, from the training perspective. It is not that these features give us answers or rules: but they strike resonances with good training practice, and with answers and rules that we have come to through other routes.

The dynamic nature of our information-processing machinery

Picture one of those see-through watches, where you can identify the mechanism inside, see the little cogs and levers and track the process that causes the hands to move. That is a static mechanism. It is built, and then it operates. Its manner of operating does not change, and cannot be influenced by 'experiences' the watch has – that is, apart from the 'experience' of being broken!

Our information-processing mechanism is not like that (and neither, just to be clear, is that of other animals). Its manner of operating evolves constantly with experience. That is how we learn. Our central nervous system is constantly establishing new connections, new pathways. I meet someone called 'Peter'. A myriad new connections are established with the place in which that name is registered in my information processor. I learn a foreign language. I forget my mother's birthday. I start practising transcendental meditation for ten minutes at the beginning of every day. All of these changes are registered by thousands of minute but co-ordinated changes in the machinery of our minds, so that every day in some way our reaction to the same information is different. In other words, every day the meaning of the same information changes.

You can see the resonance this fluid, flexible, evolving physical characteristic of our brains strikes with the points made earlier in this chapter about the power of meaning.

The machinery of our information-processing system is constantly reorganising itself around the information that has most meaning for us.

When we look at the mechanics of how information travels round our central nervous system, we are struck again by the flexibility of those mechanisms. The first nerve cells (neurons) to register a piece of information (perhaps the optic nerves registering a word on a screen) pass their message on by releasing small amounts of chemicals across minute gaps (synapses) between nerves. Different amounts of chemical trigger different probabilities of response in the next neurons in the chain. The amount of chemical released varies according to how much work the neuron has been doing, according to messages that the neuron receives from other connecting neurons which may 'inhibit' or 'excite' it (cause it to release less or more chemical), and according to patterns of reactivity which have been set up over time. So sometimes we may see but instantly forget the word on the screen, sometimes we may see it and remember it for days, sometimes we may see it and have a strong emotional reaction to it, and so on.

This flexibility of our information-processing machinery strikes resonances with our desire to provide variety as trainers, to be creative, to try a different way of getting something across if the first way does not work. There are millions and millions of opportunities to find a pathway that will work.

'Specialism' in our brains

Different physical parts of our brains have different information-processing functions. One of the most important distinctions that maps on to the way the brain is physically organised is the distinction between information from different senses. Visual information, for example, is dealt with at the back of our cerebral cortex (see Box 4 for definitions of some terms describing particular areas of the brain); auditory information is processed further forward. So the distinction between the senses continues to be significant even at the 'highest' level of our functioning (that is, in the areas of our brain that are concerned with associating ideas, learning, reasoning).

This fact about the physical structure of our information processor resonates with our instinct as trainers to get information across through as many sensory channels as we can. It is likely that different people will have more highly developed information-processing capability in different parts of their brain (and indeed there is evidence for this). So to give ourselves the best chance of getting information across to everyone, we should say it, show it, and let people experience it. Also, since the different sensory presentations are targeting different parts of our brain, we are setting up multiple connections and increasing the chances of finding a good pathway – a pathway that will stick. There is psychological research that supports this idea directly. A Nobel prize-winning psychologist, Professor Roger Sperry, found that the more that people used different parts of their brain together, the more the use of each part benefited the other. For example, it was found that the study of rhythm helped the study of languages and that the study of languages helped the learning of bodily rhythms; that the study of music helped the study of maths, and vice versa; and so on.

A specialisation of particular interest to us as trainers is that of the right brain/left brain. For right-handed people, the left-hand side of our brain is specialised for language and for sequential, analytical, logical thought processes. The right-hand side is specialised for more creative, intuitive and often spatial thought processes (such as making a mental map of a place, answering apparently 'crazy' questions such as 'What does this workshop have in common with a pot of yoghurt?', and artistic and musical activities). Again, to give ourselves the best chance of getting information across to everyone, we should use methods that appeal to the 'right brain' as well as those that appeal to the 'left brain'. So we may ask people to

Box 4

SOME TERMS FOR IMPORTANT AREAS OF THE BRAIN

Cerebrum:	the largest, most noticeable structure in the brain; it consists of two hemispheres, separated by a clear gap but joined by bands of nerve fibres; it is the latest brain structure to have evolved, and it is involved in processing and interpreting information from our senses, decision-making, reasoning, language, and so on – all the 'higher mental functions'
Cerebral hemispheres:	the two symmetrical halves of the cerebrum
Cerebral cortex:	the surface covering of 'grey matter' that is the outer layer of the cerebrum
Cerebellum:	two hemispheres, much smaller than the cerebrum, concerned with balance, posture and movement
Brainstem:	the mass of fibres coming into the brain at its root; the brainstem also contains the nerves that control basic bodily functions such as the heartbeat, breathing and blood flow

discuss a case study on leadership (a 'left-brain' activity) and then ask them to form a human sculpture representing good leadership (a 'right-brain' activity).

In brief

- Although our principal business as trainers is behaviour change, not information transfer, it is still important for us to understand how to get information across effectively.

- The areas of psychology that are particularly relevant here are: perception, attention and short-term memory; and neurophysiology.

- Research into perception, attention and short-term memory suggests to us that we need to:
  - 'keep it simple': be careful not to present too much new 'meaning' at any one go

◻ alternate information-giving sessions with activity

◻ structure information to make it as meaningful as possible to our participants, to connect with what is already in their heads

◻ exploit 'beginnings' and 'ends' of sessions for their extra attention-getting power

◻ pay attention to the physical environment and physiological condition of our participants!

∎ The main message from the study of neurophysiology is how incomprehensibly complex is the underlying machinery of our minds. None the less, there are some thought-provoking known features of this machinery, for us as trainers. In this chapter we reflected on:

◻ the dynamic nature of our information-processing machinery: the way it constantly reorganises itself around the information that has most meaning for us

◻ the 'specialism' in our brains: the fact that different physical parts of our brains have different information-processing functions; in particular, the right brain/left brain difference underlines the importance of getting information across in as wide a variety of forms as possible.

Commitment to
Change

It is now a part of training orthodoxy that our training must be 'learner-centred', not 'subject-matter centred' and certainly not (perish the thought!) 'trainer-centred'. Yet where does our certainty that this is the right approach come from? And is there any formal psychological justification for it?

I am reminded of one of my favourite jokes.

> *Question* 'How many psychologists does it take to change a light-bulb?'
>
> *Answer* 'Only one, but the light-bulb really has to want to change.'

We would all agree that learner-centred learning is the key to ensuring commitment to change. In fact, the previous two chapters, with their focus on finding what is meaningful to the learner and letting that guide both how we develop the relationship with him and how we present information to him, lead us to this point.

But let us now look at some psychology of more specific relevance to exactly this issue: the psychology of motivation, of what makes us want to do one thing rather than another, of what drives us, and ultimately, of what leads us to want to change.

When it works

I was recently running a team development programme for the senior management team of an NHS Trust. Something about the timing of the programme, the way it had been set up, and the pain that this group of people had suffered as a consequence of their poor teamworking, meant they were totally committed to change even before I opened the first session. It was one of the most enjoyable and rewarding pieces of work I have ever done, and it was characterised by the following behaviours and feelings.

- People took every task further than I had imagined they would take it (for example, in the very first session when they were making their introductions they spontaneously included information about very personal experiences that had exerted a key determining influence over the values important to them at work).

- I had the sense of information and advice being eagerly sought from me: the team had many questions for me, and many suggestions of how I could best help them.

- The team honestly confronted how difficult it was going to be to change.

- The team thought of practical ways to overcome the difficulties, and set actions in motion accordingly.

- The team worked hard but were exhilarated at the end of the day.

When it is not working

I can contrast the experience I have just related with another team development experience, this time with a group of senior engineers in a large production company. This was characterised by:

- low levels of participation and comment; very little spontaneity

- my feeling that I was 'pushing' information and ideas at the team

- tasks done with courtesy and a basic goodwill, but with no sense of urgency or purpose
- confusion – on my part and theirs – as to where all this would lead when they were back at work.

I was left feeling I had asked this group of people to do the 'wrong work'. After all, if you give people the 'right work', they will be engaged by it.

The issues for us as trainers

There is such a contrast between the value of our training when there is commitment to change and the value when there is not, that we urgently need as much help as we can get with these issues:

- how to identify what kind of change any particular group of people will commit to most readily and most determinedly
- how to identify barriers to commitment to change
- how to turn our training programmes into environments that encourage, and do not block, commitment to change.

Insights from the psychology of motivation

I remember when I was studying psychology at university how much I looked forward to the term when we would focus on the excitingly named subject 'emotion and motivation'. At last, I thought, I will discover why I feel the way I do, and what determines my, and other people's, choices.

Unfortunately for me, most of what we learned under that heading concerned the behaviour of rats, pigeons and monkeys – even dogs – under conditions of stress, fear and a variety of punishment and reward contingencies: I seemed no nearer to understanding why I always fell in love with dark-haired boys with a penchant for loud rock music!

I tell this anecdote because it is important to recognise that psychologists have engaged in a huge amount of animal research in relation to emotion and motivation. The use of animals has come about as a solution to two difficulties: first, it would be hard to conduct ethical research in which people were subjected to extremes of emotion; second, people's emotions and motivations are very complex, and it is hard to build a step-by-step scientific model of them: perhaps if we start with animals, which are simpler, and work from there, we will do better.

Although it is important to recognise that this body of animal research exists, I am not going to describe it in this book. (There are references in References and Further Reading for those who would like to know more about it.) I shall focus on the psychologists who have tried to get to grips with *human* motivation, since they are the ones most likely to have something to say to us as trainers.

Maslow's hierarchy of human needs

One of the most clearly formulated and widely influential ways of understanding what motivates us was developed in the 1950s by a psychologist called Abraham Maslow. He had got rather tired of what seemed to him an excessive focus on people with neuroses and problems, and he decided to concentrate on 'healthy' people and their potential.

He identified what he called a 'hierarchy' of important needs – and hence a hierarchy of motivational forces that can be tapped into when we want to elicit our own or somebody else's commitment to a particular course of action. He arranged the needs in the hierarchy according to the order in which they emerged as species evolved (so the highest needs are unique to man, the lowest common to all living creatures). This order also corresponds to the order in which these needs seem to emerge during an individual person's life. Figure 2 summarises the hierarchy.

Figure 2

MASLOW'S HIERARCHY OF NEEDS

'Self-actualisation'
∎ I need to become what I'm capable of becoming

'Esteem'
∎ I need to respect myself and to be respected by others

'Love and belonging'
∎ I need to be close to and feel part of family, friends, or other social group

'Safety'
∎ I need to be sure I'm safe, sane, and able to provide for myself and my loved ones

'Survival'
∎ I need to have enough to eat and drink; I need sleep; and I need sex

Source: Mackintosh and Colman (eds) (1995)

Maslow originally thought that the need for self-actualisation did not really feature until a person had satisfied all the 'lower needs'. We can see this is not so: think, for example, of famous concentration camp survivors who, by focusing on self-actualisation in the midst of the horror of their physical situation, managed not only to survive but also to engage in creative work and thought. (Bruno Bettelheim, for example, the great child psychologist, spent 12 months in Dachau and Buchenwald: he describes this time as one that shook him out of his 'earlier dogmatic slumbers'.)

It is, however, often true that if our lower-level needs are not satisfied but could be, then anyone attempting to interest us in satisfying our higher-level needs is likely to seem fairly irrelevant. Those of us who have had to give training courses to people who fear imminent redundancy – which of course threatens their 'safety' in Maslow's terms – can easily call to mind stories that bear that out.

There are perhaps two particularly relevant points for us as trainers to draw from Maslow's theory. The first is that there is a wealth of motivations that we could tap into when we are trying to create the conditions for commitment. It seems to me that we should *not* tap into them manipulatively (for example, by subtly excluding people who refuse to complete an action plan from a group discussion, in an endeavour to awaken their need for 'love and belonging'). We *can* tap into them explicitly by inviting our participants to consider a whole range of ways in which the objectives of the training programme might meet real needs that they have. We can point out possible gains of all kinds, and let people identify those which strike home for them. For example, imagine a presentation skills programme. Possible purposes of the programme, against Maslow's hierarchy of needs, could be:

self-actualisation:	to enable you to have more influence over things that matter to you
esteem:	to enable you to take credit for your ideas
love and belonging:	to enable you to play a full part in your organisation's business development
safety:	to enable you to keep your skill-set up-to-date and increase your personal marketability
survival:	?!

The second particularly relevant point from Maslow's work is the emphasis he places on the need for self-actualisation. Where our participants see that the change or development being offered by our programmes really fits with their own primary purpose in life, with their values and the realisation of their personal potential, they will commit to it with considerable force. One of the reasons why participants often appreciate our including personality questionnaires in the programmes we run is that they offer people an opportunity to understand and explore their own potential above and beyond the constraints their employing organisation has placed on the programme objectives.

Herzberg's two-factor theory of motivation

Frederick Herzberg set out to understand what make people satisfied at work. He conducted a large number of interviews with accountants and engineers, asking them to describe times when they were dissatisfied and times when they were very satisfied.

He found that there were some things that caused *dissatisfaction* if they were absent or inadequate. These were:

- pay
- job security
- status
- working conditions
- working relationships.

But interestingly, these were not the things that *caused satisfaction* if they were present and adequate. These were a quite different set of things, namely:

- interesting work
- feelings of achieving something worthwhile
- feelings of developing, growing
- promotion and recognition accompanying any of the more 'psychological' factors above.

Herzberg called the first set of things that had to be there to prevent dissatisfaction 'hygiene factors'. He called the second set of things that could actually lead to satisfaction 'motivators'.

For us as trainers this two-factor theory gives us confidence that what we are offering in the training room has the potential to make a significant positive difference to people's working lives. So we do have access to important motivators. We can increase the interest people find in their work, help them to achieve more, and certainly offer them possibilities for growth and development. (This ties in with the importance of self-actualisation needs, which we took from Maslow.)

But Herzberg's theory also warns us to be realistic about what training can achieve when 'hygiene factors' are not right. Of course, we have little influence over those. We can, however, ensure that we acknowledge their existence and give participants a chance to express their dissatisfaction about them. They will then be better able to put those issues to one side, and engage with the training.

Rogers' conditions for personal growth

Carl Rogers was probably the third most influential psychologist to date, second only to Freud and Skinner, in the sense of guiding the thinking behind contemporary psychology. He was both an academic researcher and a psychotherapist. His central idea of person-centred counselling is one of the fundamental origins of thinking on learner-centred learning. In Chapter 6 we shall be looking further at counselling approaches and their relevance and otherwise in relation to training. For now, we just want to take advantage of Rogers' thinking on how to create the ideal conditions for commitment to personal growth.

Like Maslow, Rogers believed that we all have a fundamental drive to grow and to achieve what we are capable of. Our sense of self, and of what our self can be, is critical in determining the direction and intensity of that drive.

Rogers suggests that there are two primary influences on our sense of self, influences that are exerted mainly in childhood. The first influence is the experiences that we have as we grow up – our awareness of what we find enjoyable, painful and exciting, and our awareness of what we can and cannot do. The second influence is what others define us to be, either by what they say to us or how they treat us.

A major problem in developing ourselves arises when we experience rejection or punishment through others' reactions to an aspect of ourselves that we know from our own experience to be valid. In order to continue getting 'positive regard' from others (a primary need), we have to sacrifice expression of our true selves, and our psychological growth is stunted.

Rogers maintained that this kind of block to personal development could be lifted in a relationship where we experience unconditional positive regard – warmth and respect for us as people, regardless of what we think and do. That sort of relationship is what his person-centred counselling is intended to deliver. Rogers' view was that given enough of that condition, people will begin to grow spontaneously.

As we shall discuss further in Chapter 6, it is not our job as trainers to provide counselling experiences for people. But perhaps we can take a leaf out of the counselling book in our thinking about commitment to change. We sometimes talk and act as if we think resistance to change is the natural state of all our participants, that we have to coax, cajole, and coerce them into a bit of movement. Rogers' thinking challenges that view. It says: if trainers remove the barriers to change by making the environment unconditionally valuing, people will look after the change element themselves. It is our nature to grow and develop; it is just that other things get in the way.

This line of thinking will lead us to design and implement training that is always curious rather than judgmental about participants' reactions, that is capable of being altered in response to participants' views about what they need, and that does not focus on setting up an intricate framework of 'punishments' and 'rewards' to reinforce 'good' behaviour, but instead gives participants space to work out what they consider to be 'good'.

Let me give a concrete example of this kind of training in action. Imagine you are running a customer care programme. You have just delivered an input on 'moments of truth' *, emphasising the multiplicity of tiny interactions by which customers will judge your organisation, and how it is essential to ensure each one of those interactions is as positive for the customer as it can be. You ask participants to identify 10 'moments of truth' for their customers in a typical sale. One of the participants folds his arms. He looks at you, and then round the group. He says, 'This sounds like a philosophy of being a dogsbody. I'm damned if I'm going to ensure "wonderful moments of truth" for every one of my customers, no matter how they treat me.' If you are determined to stick to the principles in Rogers' thinking, you are likely to respond along these lines: 'Well, you're certainly right to say you don't intend to be a dogsbody. Maybe we need to think about all this a bit more. Can you give me an example of where a "moment of truth" could involve your being a dogsbody in order to give a customer a positive experience?' You would be saying this out of genuine curiosity about his position, and you would be open-minded as to where the exploration will lead. You will be hoping that if you continue to create these conditions, your participant will work out for himself a sensible way of dealing with 'moments of truth'.

---

* A 'moment of truth' is a focused experience the customer has which influences his perception of the selling organisation – for example, the expression on an assistant's face as he approaches the till, the way a complaint is dealt with, the time a delivery takes.

The idea of creating such an unconditionally valuing environment for participants is an extreme one, but then in Chapter 9 we shall look at behaviourism – another extreme idea, at the opposite end of the spectrum. You can choose your own position on that spectrum, knowing that there are psychological viewpoints to support both extremes and the infinity of points in between.

Insights from systems thinking

There is something about the phrase 'commitment to change' which implies someone trying to pull himself out of a bog by his own bootlaces: a very individualistic act, fighting against all the surrounding circumstances and constraints, and against the odds. There is something else about the phrase which suggests a 'commitment switch': if only we as trainers could find this switch and use it, how well our programmes would work!

The systems approach challenges this – and much else – in our thinking about behaviour change. Its initial proposition is gloomy: that attempts to bring about change in an individual are doomed, because the individual's behaviour as it is 'fits' with the system that he is part of. If change occurs, the system will force the change back again. The reasoning is that all the people around an individual have adapted to his usual way of behaving, just as he has adapted to theirs. When he behaves differently from what they have grown to expect, they will react with surprise, confusion, and perhaps even annoyance. There will be pressure for him to 'go back to normal'. And 'commitment to change' is irrelevant: the square peg might really want to be a round peg, but if the hole it has to fit into is square, its wants are neither here nor there.

This way of thinking about change and the difficulty of bringing it about has its origins, like the person-centred approach just discussed, in psychotherapy. The depressing outcomes of psychotherapy with schizophrenic adolescents and young adults led the therapists involved to question their individually-focused approach. In the therapeutic environment, the schizophrenic patient would make a great deal of progress; then he would spend a weekend at home with his family, and all the symptoms would return with full force. Therapists began to wonder if the family system *required* the patient to be schizophrenic. So they started researching the patterns of behaviour in families with a schizophrenic member, and they discovered that the schizophrenic behaviour was indeed often held in place by a very established set of interactions between family members. (For example, the schizophrenic patient would claim to hear imaginary voices chanting 'things are not as they seem' as a response to his parents telling him they love him, but persistently ignoring his requests for practical help.) In fact, often the schizophrenic's 'crazy' behaviour was the only 'sane' way to respond to the crazy behaviour of the family!

That is the gloomy side of the systems approach. The upbeat side is that by altering the rules that govern how the parts of the system relate to each other, you can bring about behaviour change without ever having found the 'commitment' switch. Let us explore further what this upbeat side to the systems approach has to offer us in the training context.

Every individual is a system

The systems approach encourages us to see a person as a perfectly working system. All our behaviours fit together to make a stable whole. Even behaviours we would gladly be rid of (we think) – such as smoking, losing our temper, forgetting people's names – have an important and necessary place in our behavioural whole. I remember a participant on one of my training courses who said she had been trying for years to stop biting her nails in meetings. She had tried all the classic cures: foul-tasting nail varnish, buying nice things so she wanted her hands to look good for wearing them, getting colleagues to glower at her whenever her fingers went to her mouth.

Nothing brought about permanent change.

We were talking about the systems approach to behaviour change, and suddenly she said, 'I've got it! The reason I bite my nails in meetings is that it's my way of asserting my independence. It dates right back to when I was a teenager, when it used to annoy my parents. I don't feel I have enough influence in the company, so I bite my nails as a covert way of keeping my end up!' So nail-biting was part of a system that ensured this woman 'kept her end up' without losing her job (as she might have done if she had argued in meetings, or chewed gum). She worked out that the key to stopping biting her nails was to find another behaviour to take its place: so, to cut a long story short, she ended up applying for a promotion and getting it. Nail-biting was no longer necessary in her behavioural system, and it disappeared for good.

If we see individuals as perfectly working systems, then we shall be trying for lasting behavioural change by rearranging the system so it is still working perfectly but differently. Also, we shall respect 'resistance to change' because we shall see it as the individual making sure he does not sacrifice the stability of his behavioural system for a temporary isolated change.

I recall a presentation skills workshop that I attended where one of the exercises we all had to do was shout. One of my colleagues could not shout. (And this was linked with a problem he had in projecting his voice sufficiently when presenting.) Fortunately, the trainer was alert to the idea of every individual being a perfectly working system, with all behaviours forming part of a stable and interlocking whole. She asked him to consider the following questions:

- 'What stops you shouting?'
- 'What would have to change for you to shout?'
- 'If you shouted, what would you lose?'

She discovered that his inability to shout was connected with his desire to be courteous. He considered shouting to be inconsiderate to others. When everyone in the room *asked* him to shout because it would help them when it came to their turn, he did it. So he found that he could shout and still be courteous, and that led to a small but useful change in his perfectly working behavioural system.

Every individual belongs to many systems outside the training room

Just as the trainer can help the individual to rearrange his own internal behavioural system so that change is brought about and sustained, so she can help him rearrange elements in external systems to which he belongs, to achieve the same outcome.

Key questions that will help us as trainers to keep this systems perspective are these:

■ Who outside the training room will benefit if this change occurs?

■ Who outside the training room will lose if this change occurs? (We need to help participants to work out ways to minimise such losses, or those people will block the change with their own behaviour.)

■ Who outside the training room will have to change in response to this change? What is in it for them?

Here are some examples of features of good 'systems-aware' training – ensuring that the system is ready to receive and sustain the training outcomes:

■ training people in the groups in which they work

■ involving managers as co-tutors

■ 'large event training', where as much of the system as possible is brought into the training room: whole departments, whole functions, sometimes even whole companies

■ training that also involves clients and suppliers

■ asking participants to get feedback from bosses, peers and subordinates before and after training.

If the system is committed to change – in the sense of having rearranged itself in the expectation that change will occur – then the burden of individual commitment to change is much reduced.

Insights from research into self-control

Before we leave the subject of commitment to change, we must not forget some of the truths about individuals that in many ways defy incorporation into any of the psychological models of motivation.

How do we account for a person on a diet refraining from eating a luscious piece of chocolate cake when hungry? Or how do we account for a manager suddenly deciding that he is going to change the habit of a lifetime and become more open and accessible to people? He opens his office door, rearranges his furniture to encourage discussion, starts holding staff meetings every Monday morning...

Box 5 describes a systematic investigation into the 'phenomenon' of self-control by psychologists. It shows how elusive yet how powerful self-control is.

Box 5

AN EXPERIMENT INVESTIGATING SELF-CONTROL

Consider a cigarette box devised by Azrin and Powell. This device allowed a smoker to obtain a cigarette only after a given period of time had passed, perhaps one hour. Many smokers were able to cut down on their cigarette use as the waiting period was gradually extended. But any smoker could at any time have broken the contract and sought cigarettes from other sources. This self-control device, then, could have an effect on a person only if he were committed to using it, and the behaviour change procedure could be regarded as relying on self-control only if the person were *not* restrained by others to stay with the regime. For if we could construe the taking of cigarettes only from the special box as being under environmental control – the therapist's insistence that the smoker not seek another source – the control would be external, not self-exercised.

Source: Davison and Neale (1974)

Psychologists bend and twist to try to make examples like this fit their theories. Psychoanalysts suggest there is an 'inner agent', the ego (see Chapter 9), which takes charge at times, rejecting the 'baser' impulses and spontaneously choosing a higher path. Behaviourists (of whom more in Chapter 8) suppose that the person has learned to administer internal punishments to himself that 'switch off' undesired behaviour. Systems approaches would postulate unobserved changes in one or more systems that exert influence on the individual. But none of these explanations rings true.

Perhaps it is exciting and stimulating for us as trainers that psychology has not really and finally nailed down what it is that makes us change and what it is that makes us stay the same. It means that as long as we remain open-minded and creative, we may surprise ourselves and our participants in the ways we elicit their commitment.

I would like to end this chapter with a story where all the 'rules' were broken, and yet long-lasting change ensued. I love this story because it is a strong argument against the 'rescue' mentality, to which we trainers are so often prone: the feeling that we must 'save' our participants and show them a better way. It is a paradox that what draws many of us to training is an interest in and commitment to others' development, yet in order to be good trainers we have to keep a firm rein on that interest and commitment. They can so easily get in the way of participants' own commitment. For if we as trainers care too much, we will encourage dependency and we will achieve the opposite of what we want; we will end up with participants who rely on us and our commitment rather than participants who rely on themselves and their own commitment. Given everything we have said in this chapter about the power and centrality of one's own commitment to change, we can see that this is most definitely a recipe for training failure.

The story that follows is true. It challenges us all to think very carefully before doing 'what comes naturally' when we are trying to facilitate developmental change.

Debbie's story

A depressed woman came for therapy. She had no job, no stable relationship; she was fat; her appearance was dishevelled and unkempt. She had been to therapists before, to no great effect.

In the first session, she talked about how hopeless her life was, how everything she tried went wrong, how she was just one of the unlucky ones. The therapist agreed with her.

In the second session, she began to talk about some ideas she had for changing her situation. The therapist expressed doubt that any really constructive change could occur in such a bad situation.

When Debbie arrived for her third session, she had obviously had a haircut and she was wearing a new outfit. She told the therapist she had started a diet, and had met a man at the local job club whom she liked and with whom she was going to the pub that evening. The therapist expressed scepticism and advised Debbie against getting her hopes up. She did not want her to be disappointed.

In the fourth session, Debbie announced that she had got a job and had started dating this new man. She felt happier than she had for years. The therapist said she was pleased for Debbie, but doubted that it would last.

By the sixth session, Debbie had clearly lost weight, was looking very smart, and was still enjoying her new job. She said she felt she did not need therapy sessions any longer. The therapist wished her luck, but commented that Debbie would probably be back to see her before too long, 'when things take an inevitable turn for the worse!'

Six months later, the therapist received a letter from Debbie. It read, 'I want to thank you for the positive effect you had on my life. At the time, I was so angry with you I could have hit you. But it made me determined to prove you wrong. I am engaged to be married, we are buying a house, and I have been promoted to supervisor at work. I feel better about myself than ever before, and you were part of that change.'

In brief

■ However brilliantly we train, unless our participants decide for themselves that they can and want to develop, our training is a waste of time. 'Commitment to change' is the key: our job is to create the right conditions for that commitment, and to make sure we are not unintentionally blocking it.

■ We can find insights into commitment to change in the psychology of motivation, in systems approaches and from research into self-control.

■ The psychology of motivation suggests that we need to:

☐ recognise and use the many different sources of motivation that drive different individuals

☐ recognise and use the importance of people's need to become what they are capable of becoming ('self-actualisation'): participants need to see that the development offered by our programmes fits with and supports their purpose in life, their values, and the realisation of their personal potential

☐ acknowledge that sometimes there will be important sources of dissatisfaction and resentment for our participants over which we as trainers have absolutely no influence.

■ Systems approaches suggest that we need to:

☐ understand each individual as a 'system that works': every time change is contemplated, the risk is that it will throw the system; so we need to help individuals rearrange their behavioural system so that it is different, but still works

☐ remember all the systems each individual belongs to outside the training room, and acknowledge that many if not all of those systems will be trying to keep our participants the same; take account of those systems in the way we design and deliver training.

▌ Research into self-control emphasises its power and unpredictability. It reminds us to remain open-minded and creative in our efforts to elicit commitment to change.

5

Managing the Group

Most training occurs with groups. I imagine that things have evolved this way for reasons of efficiency and cost-effectiveness; I *do not* imagine that anyone ever sat down and formally addressed the question, 'What are the positive and negative implications for individuals' learning of their being trained in groups?'

But as soon as it became standard practice to train in groups, it became a priority task for the trainer to manage the group. We plunge into this task, rather like lambs to the slaughter, generally with no training ourselves in how to do it. We get better at it, through trial and error; we have some horrible experiences with groups that go 'bad' on us; eventually we develop a style, and a whole range of instincts about what is going on in the group, about what we should avoid doing, and what we should do, to make the group context as conducive to learning as possible. Perhaps psychology can help us develop faster, with fewer painful mistakes.

In fact, psychology does have a lot to say about group behaviour, which has interested researchers considerably. It has held out the possibility – always attractive to psychologists – of general 'laws' or 'principles' governing this aspect of human behaviour. And indeed there do appear to be some fairly important things one can say with a reasonable degree of certainty about the way groups behave.

In this chapter we shall summarise the most important insights into group behaviour that the general body of psychological knowledge on this topic gives us. We shall then look at two particular formulations which I think are especially relevant to us as trainers: Schutz's and Bion's. In all of this, we shall be drawing out what the implications are for our behaviour in relation to the groups we train.

When it works

Call to mind a group you have trained recently where the dynamic of the group really helped individuals within it to learn. You will probably have noticed some or all of these things going on:

▎ people chatting to each other in a relaxed and friendly way in breaks, and at the start and end of the day

▎ people exchanging information openly about their own experiences, hopes, and concerns

▎ people providing suggestions and solutions for each other, and showing interest in suggestions and solutions provided by others

▎ willingness to form all kinds of different pairs and sub-groups when this is relevant to the activity

▎ people helping each other to stay focused on the work they need to do

▎ and above all, an atmosphere, a feeling in the room, of psychological comfort and energetic enjoyment.

When it is not working

We all have vivid memories that will never leave us of bad experiences with groups. Sometimes they do not involve us, the trainer, personally: we watch, helplessly, as a clique forms, as an individual becomes marginalised, or simply as grumpiness increases between participants as the days progress. I remember a group of traders in a merchant bank who were attending an influencing skills programme. The competitive dynamic in the group was there long before they entered the training room, and it meant that trying to win in every exercise was so important that any reflection on how they had performed was completely ruled out. Also, it would have been impossible to ask them to give each other feedback: even that exercise would have been used as another opportunity to score points off each other.

Perhaps the worst experiences of all for us, however, are the ones where the group 'turns against us'. Here is one from my early training experience, when I unwittingly took on a group dynamic well beyond my capability.

Don't kick a group when they're down

I had been asked by a group of normally quite amiable senior executives to observe a three-hour meeting they were holding and to give them some feedback at the end on how well they were functioning as a team. My first, and cardinal, mistake was that I took this request at face value: I thought they wanted to make progress as a team, even at the expense of hearing some negative feedback. (In fact, what they really wanted from me was reassurance that they were OK.)

During the three-hour meeting I sat and made notes. I soon saw a pattern that I was sure was hampering their effectiveness. First, the leader – a physically small man, but with enormous suppressed energy, an ability to talk for minutes on end, and a tendency to attack first and think later – was the only person who interrupted during the meeting. Despite the fact that in any event he spoke for three-quarters of the time, the other 10 executives sharing the other quarter between them, he still interrupted and talked over them many times; they never did this to him or to each other. Second, the meeting was not so much a meeting as a set of dialogues between the leader and each of his team. There was hardly ever any discussion and debate between team members. Third, the only person who ever made a decision was the leader.

At the end of the meeting, I got up to give my feedback. I decided to do it by asking them to analyse their own decision-making processes. They refused to do it. They said there was no process to analyse: they simply moved towards decisions as a unit, in a sort of organic way. They worked so well together, they said, that there was no longer any process or any differentiation between individuals' roles.

I was completely flabbergasted by the mismatch between this view and what I had observed. I decided to abandon subtlety and just give them the feedback straight. I described what I had seen, referring to my notes. I should say that in no way did I blame the leader for the patterns I had seen; I regard those kinds of pattern as the joint responsibility of all parties involved.

They looked at me in a rather indulgent, slightly pitying way. Then the leader said he thought I had a problem, in that I read too much into things. That was the end of my feedback – and I have to say the end of my credibility with that group.

Afterwards, one of the executives who had been most humiliated by the leader during the meeting took me to one side. 'Why did you attack John (the group leader) like that, Alison?' he asked, sounding genuinely puzzled and a little hurt. 'We're all very fond of him, you know – and he's achieved an enormous amount and doesn't get any recognition for it.'

That, in fact, was the key to the whole débâcle, and the reason why I had approached the group in totally the wrong way (resulting not only in my discomfort, of minor importance to everyone but me, but in the solidification of the group's teamworking – rather than its progress and *change* – into even more limiting and unhelpful patterns). This was a group that was engaged in a very difficult task in a very critical, uncaring organisation. Its members could not possibly handle any more criticism; what they were looking for from me was some of the recognition they felt they were owed. Had I first responded to that need of theirs, we might have had a truly productive feedback session.

I have spent some time on these stories of when it is not working because if there is a single most important message from psychology about group dynamics it is simply this: never underestimate their power. And we as trainers certainly know that we do so at our cost.

The issues for us as trainers

These kinds of experiences lead us to ask ourselves questions like these:

■ What needs drive groups to behave in certain ways? How can those needs be met constructively?

■ What are the danger signs of a group dynamic becoming destructive? How can I intervene effectively when I see those danger signs?

■ How can I keep the negative power of group dynamics at bay? How can I tap into the positive power?

■ How detached from the group should I be?

Insights from Schutz's theory

Schutz is an American psychologist who used psychodynamic approaches as the basis for the development of a diagnostic questionnaire, the FIRO-B*, which allows individuals to explore the nature and intensity of their interpersonal needs. What we are interested in here is Schutz's underpinning theory: that before a group of people can work effectively together, a fairly predictable series of interpersonal issues will need to be addressed and resolved. When these issues are unresolved, they get in the way.

---

* The FIRO-B is available in the UK through: Oxford Psychologists Press Ltd, Lambourne House, 311–321 Banbury Road, Oxford, OX2 7JH

Inclusion needs

At the beginning, everyone in the group is concerned, to a greater or lesser extent, with issues of *inclusion* or belonging. Each individual wonders:

▌ Why am I here?

▌ Do I have a place here?

▌ Will I be accepted?

▌ Is being here consistent with my identity?

As trainers, we need to resolve these inclusion issues as soon as we can in a programme. We do it by:

▌ opening the programme with introductions that allow people to establish their identity and place (Box 6 on page 78 gives some examples)

▌ making sure we use participants' names

▌ using pre-course information to reassure participants that the programme is for them

▌ checking that the room lay-out gives everyone a comfortable space, and that no one is 'on the edge' physically

▌ making constant eye-contact with everyone

▌ including late-comers as soon and as smoothly as possible.

Control needs

Once people are satisfied that they belong, control issues begin to surface. Individuals are wondering:

▌ Who is in charge?

▌ How much control do I have or want?

▌ How much control will others be trying to exert over me?

▌ How much responsibility do I want to take for outcomes? How much do I want others to take?

Box 6

INTRODUCTION TECHNIQUES

Say your name and say one thing about yourself.

Say your name and one thing about why you are here.

Get together with someone else in the group and talk about who you are and what you do. Be prepared to introduce that person to the rest of the group.

Get together with someone else in the group and talk about your hobbies. Be prepared to introduce that person to the rest of the group.

Get together in small groups and find out for each person in the group:

▮ what they most want to *get from* colleagues on the programme
▮ what they most want to *give to* colleagues on the programme.

One person should be prepared to summarise themes back to the whole group.

When people are preoccupied with the kind of issues listed at the bottom of p77 there are conflicts, tussles, and bouts of what I call psychological arm-wrestling.

Unresolved control issues can really disrupt a programme. We might be tempted as trainers to deal with them by taking very obvious control ourselves, and certainly the group will feel much more comfortable as soon as it sees that we know what we are doing and can convey that to them. But if we start controlling too much there will be a control issue between us and the group. Control issues are best dealt with obliquely, by:

▮ structuring groups and tasks so that everyone has the opportunity to contribute
▮ constantly dividing and re-dividing the big group into subgroups to distract people's attention from 'who's on top?'

- skilful facilitation of whole-group discussion
- avoiding power-based confrontations with individuals in the group (for example, if someone is persistently late, it is not the job of the trainer either to accommodate that by changing the programme or to exert pressure on him to be on time)
- defusing conflicts between group members by opening the discussion to more people, by reframing what they are saying so that both can be right (for more on this, see Chapter 7), or by moving on to new topics.

Affection needs

Although some very short and/or very content-focused programmes may manage to begin and end before 'affection' needs come into play, sooner or later most training groups will begin to wrestle with these. They are about how much true interpersonal contact and validation participants can hope to get from each other, and they centre around questions such as these:

- How open can I be here?
- How close do I want to get to the others?
- Do they feel too distant from me, or too intrusively close?
- Will I get honest feedback and personal recognition here?
- Will my self-esteem and feelings of personal worth be enhanced?

If we as trainers ensure inclusion and control issues are managed, we can step back and allow participants to explore affection issues for themselves. There are great differences between people in terms of what they are looking for here, and often great resourcefulness in terms of finding it. I am sure we have all run programmes where some or all of the participants have ended up as real friends: it is great when this happens, but in a sense it is not our business. However, we do have responsibility to ensure that energy is not diverted away from the objectives of the programme that we have promised to deliver.

Our own needs as trainers

Schutz's formulation encourages us to be aware of what happens to us as the lone trainer in front of the group. Like everyone else, we have a need to belong, a need to control, and a need to get close to others. But we have to stay detached from the group of participants so that we can help them manage *their* needs in a way that allows them to learn together. As soon as we become 'one of the lads', or determined to be boss, or desirous of making friends, we become less useful to the group. Our behaviour will be determined by our need to survive in that group – just as theirs is – and so we will lose the behavioural flexibility on which they are relying for us to dig them out of holes, to re-focus their energies, to mediate and divert.

The best way to satisfy our own needs while remaining detached is to train in pairs or small teams. We then have our own group to which to belong. Sadly, however, the norm for most of us is to be alone with the group. We need to build up a strong sense of the group we belong to, even when no other representative of it is in the room. We need to discuss programmes with colleagues before and after we run them, so they are 'in our heads' as we run them. We need to establish relationships with colleagues which mean that we can phone them at times of difficulty or success, and remind ourselves very clearly that we do belong somewhere, but not in our participants' group.

Insights from the general psychology of group behaviour

Because of the deep-seated needs we have just discussed, belonging to a group exerts a powerful influence over an individual's behaviour. Also, when an individual is trying to join a group, he will behave in 'uncharacteristic' ways if he needs to, in order to get in. This kind of influence can go to great extremes: for example, someone who would never contemplate committing a crime as an individual may readily commit a serious crime if that is the behaviour expected by the group.

Conformity

The pressure to fit in with the expectations of a group – 'conformity' – is a widely established finding in social psychological research. There have been many studies into this kind of pressure and its effects in real, fairly long-lasting groups, such as groups of football fans, gangs of girls, and dormitories of boys at summer camp. But perhaps the most thought-provoking finding for us as trainers is that pressures to conform even with a group of strangers, apparently selected at random, are strong. After all, on many of our training programmes, the groups are arbitrary and participants may have little shared past or future outside the training room. Yet even there the pressure to conform will be influencing not only what they do and say but also, critically for us, what they *perceive and understand*.

A classic experiment by a psychologist called Asch brings this point home. He put an 'innocent' subject in a room with six other people, who appeared to the 'innocent' to be subjects just like her but who were in fact in alliance with the experimenter. The experimenter told the group that the experiment was concerned with the accuracy of perception. He showed them two cards. On one card was a single line, and on the other were three lines of different lengths; one of these was the same length as the line on the first card.

The experimenter told the subjects that their task was to identify that line – that is, the line from the three-line card which was the same length as the line on the one-line card. The 'innocent' was always the fifth person in the room to choose which line was right, and so she had heard the choices of four of the experimenter's 'stooges' before she made her choice. On many of the occasions on which the experiment was run, the 'stooges' all gave the same, wrong answer (as previously instructed by the experimenter). The interesting thing was to see if the 'innocent' then conformed, or held out for the right answer.

About a quarter of the 'innocents' in the series of experiments withstood the group pressure and always gave the correct response. The remaining three-quarters conformed to the group: some of them subsequently said that they had actually *seen* the wrong line as correct. Others had seen the right line as correct, but thought their own judgement must be poor and changed it to fall in line with the group. Others knew the group was wrong, but did not want to be the 'odd one out'.

What can we as trainers do about these kinds of forces? The need to conform will often be stronger for our participants than the need to learn. This means that the earlier in our sessions we can set up group rules and norms directed towards learning, the better. For then the need to conform will be working for us, not against us. There are two key ways in which we can do this.

First, we can do it by the way we structure our programmes, by the kinds of ground rules we introduce, by the nature of the tasks we set. For example, I will often ask people to give each other positive feedback only. This sets up a powerful norm of encouraging and building on strengths – all the more powerful for being unusual. I have seen trainers in the USA (and some in the UK) encourage applause after presentations – again, a norm of appreciating others' efforts. Enforcing – gently but firmly – rules of not interrupting, of taking it in turns to speak, of questioning in an exploratory rather than a critical way, is again vital to ensuring the pressure to conform supports rather than undermines learning.

The second way to achieve it, and in my view the more powerful, is for the trainer to 'model' the behaviour she believes will be the most helpful norm for the group. Psychologists have discovered that one of the most powerful forms of social learning is imitation (and we can recognise how this way of learning goes right back to our childhood).

We can take advantage of this by behaving ourselves in the way we want members of the group to behave. If we have established rapport and built credibility (see Chapter 2), then we should be influential 'models' for our group. So if we model respect for different points of view, openness, curiosity, and determination to make sense of new information, then the group is likely to establish that kind of culture itself.

Groupthink

Psychologists have found that groups may often behave 'stupidly' – far more stupidly than any of the individuals would on their own. This happens because individual members lose their willingness to challenge assumptions and present a different view: belonging becomes more important than behaving intelligently. This phenomenon is called 'groupthink'.

The concept of groupthink is a good source of creative hypotheses for us as trainers when we are feeling disappointed with what a group is achieving. We need to ask ourselves whether the social burden of keeping the group intact is interfering with participants' ability to address the tasks. (This is much better for our training effectiveness than to start dismissing the group as 'stupid'.) What we also need to do is alleviate this social burden for our participants: give them some time and space for personal reflection, or the opportunity to work in pairs. Being in a group is a strain at times as well as energising, and we need to give people a respite.

Insights from Bion

W R Bion was a practising French psychoanalyst and psychiatrist who worked extensively with groups, and his technique won international acclaim. His most important book, *Experiences in Groups*, was published in 1961. He worked at times for the Tavistock Clinic in London. Underlying Bion's theory about the way groups work, and fail to work, are psychoanalytical concepts of transference, projection, splitting and so on (which are, of course, in their turn related to a particular view of how our psyche developed through infancy, childhood and adolescence). We shall look a little more closely at psychoanalysis as a psychological approach in Chapter 9, but Box 7 introduces the key concepts since they represent dynamic processes of which it is useful to be aware when they occur in groups.

However, even if we do not want to 'buy' the psychoanalytical package, we can gain useful insights from Bion's theory. After all, it is based on a great deal of skilled and often painful (to him) work with groups of strangers.

Work group versus *basic assumption group*

Bion drew a fundamental distinction between two types of group behaviour. Groups behaving in one way he called 'work groups'; groups behaving in the other way he called 'basic assumption groups'. The work group has a real purpose and is focused on that purpose. Its members know and feel that they are together in order to achieve that purpose. Here are some examples of work groups:

■ a football team in the middle of a challenging game
■ the people on a yacht sailing through a stormy sea
■ a management team discussing budgets for next year
■ a group of strangers on a bus trying to help a mother with two small children and lots of shopping
■ a syndicate group on a training programme conducting an energetic brainstorm.

Box 7

SOME KEY CONCEPTS IN PSYCHOANALYSIS

Transference:	the process in which an individual displaces or 'transfers' the feelings they have for a significant person in their history on to another 'innocent' party; the most widely known example of this is when a patient in psychoanalysis begins to feel towards his analyst the way he felt towards his mother or father; but many people believe transference occurs widely and that, for example, individuals in groups may start feeling towards each other the way they felt towards siblings (experiencing inappropriate feelings of jealousy, resentment or rivalry, for example)
Projection:	the process in which an individual ascribes her own traits, emotions, motivations and so on, to someone else; so for example a very angry and controlling individual may think the whole world is trying to punish and control her; typically, when projection occurs, the individual denies that those traits, emotions, and motivations belong to her at all; more recent psychoanalytic schools of thought propose that projection happens all the time and is not necessarily a sign of neurosis; we constantly and unwittingly imagine others share our beliefs, values and aspirations; in groups, many such inappropriate but natural assumptions are going on all the time and frequently lead to misunderstandings of the form: 'He must have meant to make me look small because if I'd said to somebody what he said to me I'd have been doing it to make them look small'; as trainers, we can often quietly clear up such misunderstandings as they occur, and prevent them escalating
Splitting:	this is a reaction that occurs under stress, and in which an individual copes by seeing himself (and/or others) in black or white terms; in a group, an individual might decide certain members of the group were totally malevolent towards him while others were totally 'on his side'.

A 'basic assumption group' is, in contrast, held together not by a purpose but by a set of common and interlocked feelings, which are connected with a 'basic assumption' about the group and its status that all members hold, though none articulates. Here are some examples of basic assumption groups:

■ a football team in the pub after the match, slagging off the opposition

■ the people on a yacht arguing and taking sides over who should cook dinner

■ a management team that cannot function without an external facilitator to guide its process

■ a group of men on a bus jeering at a woman

■ a syndicate group on a training programme pretending to discuss the task but really having a gossip.

It will not have escaped your notice that the examples that I have given for both the work group and the basic assumption group are the same kinds of groups, just behaving in different ways. That is because *any* group can become a basic assumption group if something happens to trigger a predominance of emotion over rationality.

The work group is on the whole healthy and productive; the basic assumption group is not. Things get done in a work group; people get damaged in a basic assumption group. So you will readily see that a vital part of our job as trainers is to establish and maintain our group of participants as a work group, prevent it deteriorating into a basic assumption group, and rescue it if it does.

First, then, we need to recognise which state a group is in. Key characteristics of the work group are these:

■ The members are clear about what needs to be done and what part each of them plays in doing it.

■ The output of the group will be fairly high.

■ The group will be ready to disband when the task is complete.

■ The group will be open to people, ideas and information from outside.

■ The group will review its own performance, and try to improve.

■ The group will acknowledge failure, and try to work out why it happened.

▌ So long as individuals are playing their part in achieving the task, there is tolerance of individual differences in style, contribution, behaviour and so on.

Danger signs of the basic assumption group are these:

▌ The group shows loss of focus in relation to the task, or an inappropriate narrow intensity and rigidity in one aspect of the task.

▌ The group performs at a much lower standard than it is capable of.

▌ The group spends more time and energy developing personal relationships than doing work.

▌ The group is hostile, defensive, or dismissive towards people, ideas and information from outside.

▌ The group perceives negative feedback as a threat, and responds inappropriately emotionally.

▌ There appear to be all sorts of unspoken rules, in-jokes, taboos, patterns of alliance, and covert communication which bear no relationship to the task in hand.

To establish and maintain a group as a work group, we as trainers need to give it relevant and interesting work that it is capable of doing. If we confuse a group with unclear instructions, threaten its self-esteem with work that is too difficult, damage its self-respect with work that is too easy or which appears to have no point, then we push it towards becoming a basic assumption group. We also need to provide plenty of organisation and structure round the relevant and appropriate work: without organisation and structure, the slide through confusion to fear and finally to basic assumption is always likely.

Of course, groups often turn into basic assumption groups through no fault of ours, the trainers. They may become that way because the organisation has made them fearful, or because something threatening happens while they are on the programme (another organisational restructuring, the announcement of bonuses, a worrying development in the marketplace). Then the lifeline we must throw them to draw them back towards work-group status is, once again, clear, relevant and engaging work that it can do. I once saw a trainer conducting an appraisal skills workshop with university lecturers. They arrived as a basic assumption group; they were angry and hurt at recent changes to their pay-scale. In fact they arrived united around the assumption that the trainer was going to be the enemy, demonstrating his lack of respect and understanding for their world with a flood of management-speak about 'performance'. He immediately realised the work he had planned was not the work they needed, and decided to ask them to design their own work for the day. He gave them just these three constraints:

■ They should work together as a group all day.

■ The work should enhance the lecturers' ability to learn from, coach and mentor their colleagues, and those who worked for them.

■ The work should make use of him, the trainer, as a resource to the group in some way.

By the end of the day, this group of lecturers had designed a system for peer appraisal which they planned to put forward to the university management committee. They had certainly spent most of the day as a work group.

Different kinds of basic assumption groups

Bion identifies three kinds of basic assumption group: the dependency group, the fight/flight group, and the pairing group. Here are their different basic assumptions.

Type of group	Basic assumption
■ dependency	they need a leader or some other external force to 'save' them
■ fight/flight	what matters most is the survival of the group, and that survival is under constant threat
■ pairing	the group exists to facilitate individuals in it pairing off.

The need to avert these different kinds of basic assumption group presents us as trainers with some different challenges (in addition to the overall challenge to maintain the group as a work group).

We need to be wary of the group's becoming dependent on us. If they rely on us for answers and for feedback rather than on each other, then we are not helping them to achieve all they are capable of. Also, we are colluding in the evolution of an artificial world, which will disappear together with most of the learning it engendered, as soon as we walk away.

It is in part to avoid encouraging dependency group behaviour that many of us prefer not to give feedback at all as trainers, leaving it to the members of the group to give feedback to each other.

We also need to watch out for the group's seeing us as the enemy (fight/flight). This does *not* mean we have to curry favour with the group – quite the reverse. The best way to avoid becoming an enemy is to establish a detached neutral status, as free as possible from emotional charges between us and the group. We can be funny, we can be lively, we can be considerate and interested; but we should not be emotionally involved. I do know trainers – and some very skilled ones – who get overtly angry with groups. Personally, I think it is a risky path.

Finally, we need to do whatever we can to keep professional the relationships in the groups with which we work. Really, the only way we can influence this is through our own behaviour: if a group decides to become a pairing group, there is little a lone trainer can do to counter such an irresistible force of nature! She just needs to continue presenting the relevant, interesting and doable work.

Insights from encounter groups

Before we leave this important topic of managing the group, we should pause to consider the school of psychology where people are brought together in groups specifically to elicit group dynamics: the encounter group movement. (Bion's work was conducted under this general umbrella.) We as trainers should consider it for two reasons. First, it may give us some more ideas about the kind of positive experiences that being trained in a group can bring, so that we can recognise and enjoy them when they occur, and encourage them in small ways. Second, it should help us to be clear, for our own sake and our participants', about the kinds of group we are *not* running.

Encounter groups are brought together for the purpose of promoting the personal growth of all the members. About a dozen people, usually with a 'facilitator' or leader, meet either regularly or for one long intensive session, perhaps lasting over a weekend. Their interest is likely to be in personal development or some aspect of their relationships with others. The aim is to provide a caring environment where members of the group can feel free to share whatever thoughts and feelings they wish. It is an opportunity to explore together how members feel about themselves and about each other – and simply belonging to an encounter group can be a nurturing experience.

Groups are usually composed of strangers, but sometimes members are drawn from the same environment or work setting. (In fact, there was a craze in the 1960s for holding these kinds of groups in organisations instead of various sorts of interpersonal skills training; there was then a backlash against 'playing at psychotherapy' in the workplace.)

The possibility of getting and giving honest feedback from a range of people, of learning about others' ideas and perspectives with no need to experience these as either competitive or threatening, and of enjoying a group experience while achieving useful work: these are things we can strive to mirror in our training.

However, we need to be aware that if we are not clear at all times about the boundaries of the work to be done, participants might accidentally start behaving *as if* they were in an encounter group. After all, sitting in a training room feels much more similar to being in an encounter group than it does to doing a normal day's work at the office. So we should be alert for inappropriate levels of disclosure, and emotion inappropriate to our skill as trainers, to our contract with our participants, or to the organisation's contract with its employees. When such disclosure or emotion occurs we need to draw a safe box around it and move the group back on to the work. I recall, for example, a programme on coaching skills that I ran where one manager disclosed that one of the reasons he found it so difficult to coach his employees was that his own father had had a particularly controlling, tyrannical style of 'teaching' him when he was a child. I had to draw a safe box round that disclosure by generalising from it ('It is true that our own experiences of being coached, particularly when we're young, are very influential on our style as coaches'), by inviting others to share similar but slightly less personal examples ('Can we just find out what other bad experiences of coaching people in the room have had? Maybe even in this organisation?'), and by moving on to the next piece of work ('Now I'd like you to identify something you know how to do which you would like to coach one of your colleagues in').

In brief

■ Managing the group is a key 'housekeeping' task for trainers. Unless we do it well, problems with group dynamics will totally eclipse our training agenda. Also, if we do it well the group dynamic will act as a powerful incentive to learning. Yet most trainers receive little or no formal training in how to manage groups.

■ Psychologists have studied group behaviour over a long period of time and in considerable depth.

■ The general psychology of group behaviour suggests that we need to:

- ☐ understand the tremendous pressures to conform that being in a group exerts
- ☐ use these pressures positively by setting up group rules and norms directed towards learning – explicitly, through the ground rules and structure of the programme; and implicitly, by behaving ourselves in the way we want members of the group to behave
- ☐ remember that being in a group is at times a strain for our participants.

- ▮ Schutz's theory of interpersonal needs suggests that we need to:
  - ☐ help participants to reassure themselves, as close to the start of a programme as possible, that they have a rightful place in the group and that their individual identity will be acknowledged throughout
  - ☐ ensure that struggles for control do not get in the way of learning
  - ☐ manage our own interpersonal needs so that they do not get in the way of our effectiveness as trainers.

- ▮ Bion's psychodynamic work with groups suggests that we need to:
  - ☐ establish and maintain our group of participants as a work group, with clear, relevant and interesting task objectives
  - ☐ rescue the group when it deteriorates, often through no fault of its own, into unfocused emotion
  - ☐ use structure and organisation to achieve these things.

- ▮ An examination of the encounter group movement reminds us of the positive benefits that being trained in a group can bring, but it also warns us to steer clear of inappropriate psychotherapeutic interventions. We have to make the group experience as safe as we can for the participants.

6

Counselling the Individual

In the last chapter we focused on the psychology of *groups*, and on our role as trainers in managing the group. In this chapter, we turn our attention to the psychological approaches that have most to say about how we can help *individuals* achieve the change they want by 'counselling' approaches. (We have of course already included reference to counselling approaches elsewhere in this book, for they permeate most of the psychology that is relevant to training, but here we shall look at them more explicitly and directly.)

Although we generally train groups rather than individuals, part of the measure of our success is our ability to build an effective relationship with each individual in the group. Each person learns in a different way, has a different set of priorities, and a unique set of resources to draw on. Even when we are talking with the group as a whole, we need to have an image in our mind that we are conducting a whole set of simultaneous conversations with each individual. (Interestingly, the better we have done our job in managing the group, the freer each individual in it will be to use the training to achieve his own personal goals in his own way.)

We also have time as trainers to spend with individuals. We will generally be talking with individuals at break times, and during the evening on residential programmes. We may have structured the programme itself to allow short periods for us to work with individuals. Sometimes a participant will seek us out with a pressing individual issue in relation to the content of the training. Sometimes someone will ask for our help on something unconnected with the training, which our presence as someone neutral, helpful and skilled in helping people to develop has brought to the surface.

Finally, many of us provide one-to-one coaching and 'role counselling' work as part of our portfolio of training and development activities.

For all these reasons, the area of counselling the individual is relevant to us, and psychology has some useful things to say about it.

When it works

A colleague was part of a team conducting a week-long residential programme on strategic management skills with a group of executives from a large public-sector organisation. As part of this programme, the participants were profiled on a range of psychometric questionnaires. The tutors were available to give participants individual sessions in the evenings on anything of interest or concern to them arising from their profiles; all the participants took advantage of this.

My colleague spent an hour one evening with one executive who had been particularly struck by the indications on his profile that he was a strongly 'introverted' thinker (see Chapter 2, page 21 for a definition). It tied in with some feedback he had had from his team that they never quite knew what he was thinking, and that they found him rather intimidating. (He was, incidentally, also very *tall*, well over six feet!) He felt it was not helpful that his team found him intimidating, and he wanted to lead them in a more open, relaxed way. My colleague was able to help him think of ways to achieve this.

This kind of individual counselling can be a really useful part of a training programme for participants. Not only that, it makes the group sessions more productive because individuals are developing their own personal agendas for learning and these are beginning to drive them more than group pressures to conform (see previous chapter).

The characteristics of this kind of individual counselling, when it happens in a way that is appropriate to the training context, are these:

▌ The areas that people want to discuss are related to the content of the training.

▌ They have clear goals for the discussions, and make some progress in a fairly short time.

▌ The trainer has these kinds of conversations with a range of participants.

When it is not working

We can contrast that kind of positive experience with the experience we have when we get enmeshed in a participant's personal issues. We can accidentally find ourselves lured into a helping situation which is beyond our competence – and also outside the explicit contract we have with participants and with their organisation. Also, when we are not managing the group effectively so that participants are learning from each other, we can become the sole source of help, completely overloaded by individuals queuing up to see us.

The issues for us as trainers

So the sorts of questions we trainers hope psychology will give us some answers to are these:

▌ Should I steer clear altogether of anything which smacks of 'counselling'?

▌ How can I draw the right kind of boundaries around what I can help individuals with and what I cannot?

▌ What sorts of counselling approaches are most

appropriate for me as a trainer to have as mental models?

- What sorts of counselling skills are most relevant to me as a trainer? Are there any I can use in individual sessions that will not get me 'in too deep'?

Insights from definitions of counselling

In many ways, counselling has achieved a much more self-confident and self-conscious identity than has training. Although there is a plethora of different counselling approaches and philosophies – differences that provoke outright hostility between their various proponents! – there has been a great deal of discussion and debate about what counselling is, what it is for, and who should do it. It is interesting for us as trainers to look at some of the conclusions that counselling professionals have come to about the identity of their discipline, and to compare and contrast it with our own. Through doing this, we gain insights into what training is, what training is for, and what it is not.

Definitions that highlight the difference between counselling and training

Freud was reported to have said that the goals of psychoanalysis are to:

- help patients to work and to love
- turn neurotic misery into ordinary human unhappiness.

Many people would regard counselling as being about the alleviation of psychological pain, and the 'cure' of neuroses ('neurosis' is itself an interesting psychological concept, so I have defined it more fully in Box 8).

Another definition of counselling, which places less emphasis on 'psychic sickness' is that it is:

- a relationship by means of which counsellors help their clients to live more effectively and to cope better with their problems of living.

Box 8

THE PSYCHOLOGICAL CONCEPT OF 'NEUROSIS'

A neurosis is a personality or mental disturbance not due to any known physical cause. Freud was originally responsible for the widespread use of the concept. In psychoanalysis, the term is used to indicate the underlying psychological anxieties and conflicts that lead to observed symptoms that the patient wants 'cured'. So, for example, if I have a panic attack whenever I see a river, a psychoanalyst might suggest (after appropriate exploration, of course!) that this was caused by an underlying fear of losing control, ultimately deriving from a destructive relationship with my tyrannical and manipulative father. The neurosis is the extreme fear of losing control; the symptom is panic attacks at the sight of moving water.

The problem with the concept of 'neurosis' is its virtually universal applicability combined with its unprovability. You can accuse anyone, and indeed yourself, of all kinds of neuroses to 'explain' undesirable behaviour. But you may simply be imagining things, or projecting on to others your own beliefs about why people behave the way they do. Also, identifying a 'neurosis' does not necessarily bring you any closer to a 'cure'.

I have also heard the aim of counselling described as 'to make people happier'.

These definitions immediately make us aware that what we are doing as trainers is quite different from trying to 'cure' neuroses – and they also suggest to us some boundaries around what we do. If participants ask us to step outside these boundaries, we need to identify some other source of help for them.

▌ As trainers we are not concerned with all-embracing goals, such as 'to help people to work and to love'; we have specific contracts with our participants, with much more bounded objectives, such as 'to give managers the skills and confidence they need to confront performance issues with staff constructively', we may have personal values as trainers which go beyond the narrow objectives of each programme, but they belong to us and not to training and so we may cherish but must not indulge them.

▌ We are not in the business of 'curing' anyone. If people are in psychological pain or distress, it is our job as fellow human beings to help them find someone who can help them; it is not our job as trainers to do it ourselves.

▌ We are not in the business of making people happier or more effective in their lives as a whole. We hope that people will enjoy our courses and learn a variety of useful things, but we should not set out intending to change their lives in any way, no matter how positive that intention might be.

I think it is a relief that as trainers our boundary excludes these kinds of relationships with our participants. It is quite hard enough work getting across what we need to get across, facilitating learning on the appropriate topic, and managing the dynamic forces of the group effectively!

Definitions that highlight the similarities

Despite everything I have said above, there are other ways of looking at counselling that allow us to see what training has in common with it. Here is one such.

> Counselling aims to help clients… to help themselves. The counsellor's repertoire of psychological skills includes both those of forming an understanding relationship with clients and also skills focused on helping them to change specific aspects of their feeling, thinking and behaviour.
>
> Nelson-Jones (1983)

Also, many definitions of counselling emphasise the goals of personal growth and development. These emphases on developmental change, facilitated by a third party but fundamentally determined by the individual himself, are very familiar to us as trainers.

Insights from the variety of counselling approaches

Before we look at any particular counselling approaches in detail, let us acknowledge the huge variety of counselling approaches there are. Here are just some of the extremes:

■ Ask a client to lie on a couch, sit behind him, and ask him to tell you his dreams and free associations. Every so often, offer an interpretation of what they mean.

■ Get a client and her entire family into a room with you. Encourage them to talk to each other, watch what happens, and intervene so that they understand each other better.

■ Sit down opposite a client and discuss his problem with him, questioning him in a way which leads him to a solution.

■ Find out what your client is afraid of; teach him relaxation techniques; introduce first the idea of what he is afraid of, then a picture, then the real thing, all the time helping him to use the techniques you have taught him to stay relaxed (you can read more about this technique in Chapter 9).

■ Hypnotise your client.

■ Reward your client for 'good' behaviour, punish her by withholding attention or deducting 'points' for 'bad' behaviour.

Even within each school of counselling there is a huge range of therapists with different styles. In family therapy, for example, there is Salvador Minuchin who typically engages a family member as a co-therapist; Carl Whitaker who sometimes falls asleep as a message to the family; Virginia Satir who asks families to create living sculptures to portray their relationships; Paul Watzlawick who instructs families to do the opposite of what he thinks they should; and so on.

While some of these counselling approaches have no place in the training room, I think there is a message in all this diversity for us as trainers. It is that the things we can do to facilitate behaviour change are many and various; that there is no one right way; that we can experiment and choose what suits us; and, above all, as summarised so eloquently in the basic tenets of neurolinguistic programming:

> If something isn't working, do something – anything – different.

So in that spirit, let us examine a little more closely the aspects of counselling that are most relevant to us as trainers.

Insights from listening and questioning techniques

If a time and motion specialist were to come and observe what we actually do as trainers, I think that near the top of the list of activities he compiled would be 'listening' and 'questioning'. In counselling psychology, more than anywhere else, techniques of listening and questioning have been studied and developed, and much learned about which techniques have which effects.

Precision questioning versus *fuzzy questioning*

Imagine that someone said to you, 'I want to stop getting so nervous before making a presentation.' You might respond with a whole series of 'precision questions' like these:

▌ How exactly do you feel when you are nervous? How would you like to feel different? Where is the physical sensation located?

▌ How soon before a presentation do you get nervous? What triggers it?

▌ What is the most nervous you have ever been? Tell me about that occasion. What is the least nervous you have ever been? Tell me about that.

▌ What do you mean by 'presentation'?

▌ Do you want to be completely relaxed? Or just a little less nervous?

And so on.

Or you might respond with a fuzzy question, like this:

▌ Why are you feeling like this?

Counselling psychologists draw a strong distinction between these two types of question because they have discovered that they have quite different effects. They are both valuable techniques, depending on what you are trying to achieve. Precision questioning leads to much clearer understanding on the part of both questioner and respondent about what the respondent means. It also allows the questioner to help the respondent by guiding his thinking down a particular structured path, usually calculated to reach some new insight and/or plan for change. The questioner comes across as clear-thinking and helpful – the respondent is inclined to follow her down the path.

Fuzzy questioning, however, throws the ball right back to the respondent. It almost encourages him to go on free-associating to his original statement, to generate whatever information comes bubbling up to the surface of his consciousness. The questioner is stepping right back, to learn more.

I think we often spend too much time as trainers in precision questioning, too little in fuzzy questioning. And that is one of the habits that can lead us to end up with the responsibility for the learning that occurs in the room. We can use fuzzy questions to hand that responsibility back, because the implicit message is that we are not sure where to go next, but perhaps someone else is. It is certainly good to have both techniques in our repertoire.

Fuzzy questioning is particularly useful when we want to get others involved in a discussion – when we want participants to learn from each other. We can throw out fuzzy questions like these:

- What does anyone else think about it all?
- How is anyone feeling just now?
- Where do we think this is taking us?

We generally understand precision questioning. We have learned how to do it on interviewer skills training programmes, calling it 'the funnel' and 'probing'. And we are diligent about it, because we take seriously our responsibility to be clear.

But counselling psychology suggests that we also have a responsibility to be unclear sometimes, if we are trying to help people help themselves. I know a therapist who always starts his first session with a client with that fuzziest of questions: 'What ails?'

In that way, he knows he will hear what the client wants to tell him, and not what the client has deduced he wants him to say. The brilliant family therapist Carl Whitaker is famous for his obscure, puzzling responses to things the family says: by being fuzzy to the point of craziness, he challenges them and puts them in touch with less familiar parts of themselves. He uses humour, indirection, boredom and even falling asleep – so that people will work hard to find their own meaning, rather than wait for him to give it to them.

As trainers, we are not licensed, either literally or metaphorically, to go so far. But we do need to take the lesson from counselling psychology that being crystal clear is only one technique.

The power of listening

As trainers, we are often very conscious of the need to do something, to get something across, to put things in another way that might be more helpful, to *train*, in fact. Counselling psychology reminds us that often by raising an issue for consideration and then simply listening, with all our intelligence and all our respect for other people's views, we can achieve, or more importantly help our participants to achieve, as much if not more.

Counsellors have some very specific active listening techniques, which are a useful part of any trainer's repertoire. One is that of 'reflecting', where we repeat what someone has said, in our own words so they know we heard what they meant, but without adding to or detracting from the meaning. A participant might say: 'I've been on loads of assertiveness courses, but I still can't say "no" to my boss.' A reflecting response would be: 'So you haven't found assertiveness training has helped you say "no" to your boss.'

If you recall what we said about 'pacing' in Chapter 2, about assuring participants that our starting point is their map of reality and not our own or somewhere else altogether, then you will readily appreciate the value of some reflecting comment.

'Summarising' is similar to reflecting – in that you do not distort the meaning of what has been said – but it is a technique that builds a bridge between finding out about something and going on to respond in some way. Typical summarising statements begin like this.

- As I hear it, the main issue is...
- So your primary concern is...
- You have made three important points there – first... second... third...
- So in short, you feel this....

Summarising is a very important skill for us as trainers. One of our most important tasks is to manage time effectively, not letting the group get stuck in unproductive discussions. Summarising enables us to draw a line under a discussion, satisfy participants that we have heard their view, and get their tacit permission to go forward.

Insights from 'solution-focused brief therapy'

When people undertake classic psychoanalysis, they are typically signing up for five years or more of three to five one-hour sessions a week. It seems self-evident that this overall counselling approach has little to offer the trainer. Its frame of reference is entirely different (although the models and theories that underpin it are of interest to us, and we explore them in Chapters 5, 7 and 9).

The counselling approaches that are likely to be most relevant for us to borrow from are those that focus on dealing with specific issues in a short time-frame. The most straightforward example of these is 'solution-focused brief therapy'.*

Focus on solutions, not problems

In solution-focused brief therapy, clients do not spend a lot of time trying to understand their problem. The assumption is that successful work depends on knowing where the client wants to get to. Once this is known, the task of the counsellor is to help the client find the quickest way there.

So to go back to our earlier example of someone who comes up to us and says 'I want to stop getting so nervous before making presentations', we might say, 'How would you like to feel before making presentations?' and go from there. You can see how different this approach is from one that begins, 'Why do you think you get so nervous?' and how in many ways it is much more appropriate to a training context.

---

* For further information and courses, contact: Brief Therapy Practice, 77 Muswell Avenue, London N10 2EH

Exception-finding

I really like this as a technique because it stops us getting hypnotised by our incompetence and reminds us there is a life beyond, outside, and in spite of some particular piece of incompetence. So when someone raises a 'problem' – something they want changed – do some 'exception-finding' by asking questions like these:

▌ Can you tell me about the times this *does not* happen?

▌ When are the times it bothers you *least*?

▌ What was life like before you had this problem?

Then you can go on to ask:

▌ What are you and others doing differently at those (exceptional) times?

You can use 'exception-finding' to lift a group out of purposeless complaining. I recall once working with a group of managers who were stuck in complaining about 'top management'. I lifted them out of that by asking – and it was genuinely meant, not a ploy – 'Can you think of any instances where top management have shown they're *worth* their position and pay-packet?' The discussion became much more productive from that point on, and led to some important insights into what kind of support could be expected from top management, and what could not.

Locating resources, building on strengths

Solution-focused brief therapy assumes that people already have the resources they need to solve most of their problems; they just cannot always access them. Given that a preoccupation of trainers is how to get people to take charge of their own development (remember Chapter 4 has more on this), this assumption of competence is very apposite.

The sorts of questions this therapeutic approach provides for helping people to gain access to their resources are these:

- When you faced this sort of problem in the past, how did you resolve it?
- How could you do that again?
- What other tough situations have you handled?
- What is your approach to finding solutions to tough situations?
- When you have had to deal with people like this in the past, how have you done it?

Constructive feedback

In solution-focused brief therapy, a primary role of the counsellor is to notice anything that might contribute to the client reaching his goal. This can be reported behaviour, attitude during the session, responses of other people, evidence of survival, determination and perseverance. The more the client is told of what is noticed, the more aware he becomes of the resources he has, and the more likely he is to use them. Comments like these by the counsellor are typical:

- Have you always been a survivor or did you have to learn the hard way?
- How do you manage to keep your sense of humour – is this one of the qualities that has kept you going?
- Is this determination not to give up typical of you?

As trainers, we could do a lot worse than to identify in our participants what they are already doing right in relation to the training goal, and to encourage them to do it more.

Feedback and the Johari window

Asking participants to give each other feedback is so much the stock-in-trade of every trainer and every training programme that we may sometimes be led into doing it routinely, almost thoughtlessly. Counselling psychology reminds us to be careful.

It is clear that people's level of self-awareness, and their awareness of their impact on others, varies hugely. The reasons for the variation are deep-rooted. If there is one thing counselling psychology teaches us more than anything else, it is that each of us must protect our own self-esteem if we are to function. So we can afford to allow ourselves to see only *some* things about ourselves and about what others think about us. The whole truth – whatever that might be – could well destroy us. In fact, one reason why psychoanalysis typically takes so long and is conducted in such a careful, almost formulaic way, is that it aims to give us an unrivalled degree of insight into who and what we really are. That is dangerous.

So we are at risk when we receive feedback from others. Which of us does not know that sense of apprehension, when we know someone is about to give us feedback? And as trainers we also see it in our groups.

There is a model for understanding both the aims of feedback and the differing degrees of readiness for it that derives from counselling psychology. It has already been adopted enthusiastically by the training profession, so useful is it in helping participants to manage the feedback they give and receive that it is helpful, not harmful. It is called the 'Johari window', after the two people who developed it (Joseph Luft and Harry Ingham), and it is illustrated in Figure 3 on page 108.

If the whole window represents the whole truth about us, then the four quadrants represent the following parts of that truth:

▮ The 'open' window is all those things that I know and which other people also know – for example, that I have curly hair, I studied psychology, or I am writing a book. ('Others' in this model refers to the people one is with at the time of thinking about the Johari window – not to everyone in the world!)

▮ The 'blind' window is things I do not know about myself but which others do – for example, that I have

Figure 3

THE JOHARI WINDOW

	True things about me known by me	True things about me not known by me
True things about me known by others	'open'	'blind'
True things about me not known by others	'façade'	'unconscious'

a ladder in my stockings, that I am repeating material everyone has heard before, or that the way I introduced the course worked really well for the group.

■ The 'façade' represents things I know about myself but either have not yet disclosed or have actively concealed – for example, that I have given this course ten times before, that I hate air-conditioning, or that I am anxious about the session on stress management.

■ The 'unconscious' represents things that are true about me but which no one, including me, knows. Usually things in the unconscious window are the stuff of therapy proper – not things that training courses should deal with.

People vary greatly in terms of how big their 'open window' is. And the size of the open window will be determined by their need to protect their self-esteem. Robust individuals, in this respect, have a huge open window and are constantly disclosing things about themselves and seeking feedback. More fragile individuals keep their open window small.

The most useful kind of feedback is feedback that increases the size of the open window and reduces the size of the blind window. But the most useful kind of feedback is also feedback that does this in a way and at a pace appropriate to the original size of the open window. If you give people too much, too fast, or on subjects that are too sensitive, they will either have to shut their ears to it or risk a collapse of their self-esteem.

You can make sure that feedback is appropriate in this way by taking the following steps:

- Give participants the opportunity to *ask* for feedback on particular things rather than have it forced on them by the free choice of the person giving feedback: people will generally ask for the feedback they can cope with.
- Watch for literal signs of 'closing up' that tell you the feedback is too much (turning away, looking away, interrupting, folding arms, crossing legs, etc).
- Talk to participants about the Johari window before you ask them to give each other feedback; this will make them more sensitive to self-esteem issues.

Insights from the ethics of counselling

The dictionary defines 'ethics' as 'principles of conduct', and links them with morality. I am not sure this adequately captures the nature of the ethical issues we face as trainers. So let me summarise three training scenarios, all of which have been experienced recently by me or by trainers I know.

First, you have been engaged to run a teambuilding programme for a senior manager and her direct reports. She is paying you, and is your primary client. Following the programme, she arranges a review meeting with you at which she asks for your view on each of her team. She is also thinking of moving one individual out of the team, because 'he just does not seem to be a teamplayer'. She wants your advice. What do you do?

Second, during a presentation skills workshop you, the tutor, notice signs of extreme stress in a participant. Others on the workshop take you to one side and tell you that comments this individual has made during breaks suggest he is on the verge of a nervous breakdown as a result of a very destructive relationship with his boss. They urge you to help. Do you get involved?

Now imagine that you are working with a group on assertiveness training. Participants are describing occasions when they wish they had stood up for themselves more. You have some relevant experiences too. Do you share yours, or is that crossing a boundary unhelpfully?

The scenarios cover:

■ the issue of confidentiality of information gained in a training context (the first two scenarios)
■ the issue of self-disclosure: how much can and should the trainer reveal about herself to the group (the third scenario)?

I am sure that reading through these scenarios has immediately brought more of the same to your mind: situations where you had to make a decision, based on your values and your sense of right and wrong, where different people might reasonably hold different views on what you should do.

Let us see what counselling psychology has to tell us about these two issues of confidentiality and self-disclosure.

Confidentiality

Because people in the counselling context need to be more open than they would normally be about themselves and their lives, counsellors have given a lot of thought to confidentiality issues. Issues of confidentiality are dealt with explicitly right at the start of any counselling relationship. The counsellor will say to whom and under what circumstances she will disclose information, and guarantee that, apart from that, everything that happens in the counselling room is confidential to her and the client. As trainers we certainly need to be at least as explicit, and at least as sensitive to the implications of sharing any information outside the context in which it was gained.

Self-disclosure

Counsellors have also thought about and discussed at length issues concerning how much they tell clients about themselves. It is interesting for us as trainers to gain some insight into how they think about this, since we have to make decisions all the time about how much to talk to the groups we are working with about our own personal experience and attitudes.

Counsellors adopt positions on self-disclosure along the whole spectrum, from revealing nothing to sharing just about anything. Psychoanalysts keep themselves to themselves (to encourage the development of transference – see Box 7 (page 85) – and inhibit the development of counter-transference, where they as analysts start feeling towards the client as they feel towards significant people in their own lives). More humanistic counsellors on the other hand will sometimes share intimate information about themselves if they think it will help.

I have seen trainers operate along a similar spectrum, but I have often wondered whether this is as a result of a conscious professional decision or is just the result of different trainers' personalities and preferences. In order to make a conscious professional decision more of the time, we can ask ourselves the following questions when we are contemplating self-disclosure (these questions are drawn from thinking on the subject in counselling psychology):

▐ Will I be modelling a useful skill (for example, giving specific, relevant feedback)?

▐ Will I be demonstrating genuineness?

▮ Will my experiences be helpful because they really are similar to the participant's?

▮ Will I be being open about my opinions and feelings in a way that will help participants make up their own minds?

▮ Will I be being firm and setting some useful limits?

If the answer to any of these questions is 'yes', then self-disclosure may be appropriate, depending on the answers to the next set of questions.

▮ Will I be burdening other people with my issues?

▮ Will I be dominating the session too much – will it make the session too 'trainer-centred'?

▮ Will I come across as weak or unstable?

▮ Will I be making myself inappropriately vulnerable?

If the answer to any of *these* questions is yes, then it will probably be better to hold back.

In brief

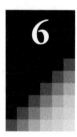

▮ As trainers, we are often asked to provide developmental advice, help and support to individuals. Even though we are usually dealing with groups, it is the individuals in the group, and their personal developmental journeys, which matter. So we need to look to counselling psychology for guidance on how to do our job effectively.

▮ Definitions of counselling remind us that trainers are *not* counsellors: our work with people focuses on specific objectives explicitly agreed not only with participants but with their employing organisations.

▮ We are, however, like counsellors in that we are concerned with self-determined developmental change.

▮ Listening and questioning techniques used in counselling suggest that we need to:

- ☐ use both probing, 'precision' questioning and vague, 'fuzzy' questioning, at different times, and for different purposes
- ☐ remember how much we can achieve simply by listening.

▌ Solution-focused brief therapy approaches remind us to:

- ☐ focus on solutions rather than problems
- ☐ concentrate on mobilising the innate resourcefulness of people to solve their own problems
- ☐ give constructive feedback whenever and wherever possible.

▌ The 'Johari window' reminds us that the best kind of feedback is feedback that is actively sought by the recipient and so matches what they personally can 'take'.

▌ The ethics of counselling emphasises the importance of our addressing ethical issues as we develop our training style.

▌ The variety of counselling approaches encourages us always to be prepared to try something different, if what we are doing is not working.

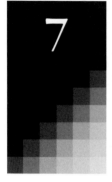

7

Handling Conflict

It is hardly surprising that at times conflict occurs during training. Given the group dynamics which the training environment creates (see Chapter 5) and the fact that the subject matter of training is often controversial, it is perhaps surprising that conflict does not happen more often. Also, all of us know that the training room is a place where people sometimes take the opportunity to express their anger or frustration at the organisation that employs them, at their bosses, and at their paymasters of various kinds. There is something about the training agenda that triggers this. Personally, I think it is because most participants are at least a little bit suspicious that they are being 'sent' on a training course because they have been judged deficient in some way. They are determined to redress the balance by expressing their feelings about other people's deficiencies.

Anyway, for all these reasons, conflict bubbles under the surface and emerges from time to time. We as trainers need to know how to cope with it and how to use it constructively. Where there is conflict, there is energy; where there is energy, there is the possibility of growth.

Let us just be clear about what we mean by 'conflict' before we go any further. As we shall discover, it is a term laden with all kinds of meanings in psychology, some of them quite abstruse. What I mean here is: a clash between people, caused by antagonistic views or wishes, and accompanied by strong feelings.

When it works

We do not have to go far in our accumulated experiences of training to identify times when the energy caused by conflict was turned to positive outcomes.

Just one example of this occurred recently in a training programme I was observing. The programme was on creative thinking skills, and by the time it had got to the afternoon of the second, and final, day people's energy was beginning to flag.

During the two days, a split had emerged between the smokers and the non-smokers. Of the 10 participants, three were smokers. They not only went outside to smoke during breaks but often chose to work together in the group exercises so that they could do them outside and be free to smoke then too. It was clear to me observing (and also to the trainer, who was not a smoker, and spent his break-time inside with the non-smokers) that there was a degree of suspiciousness about the smokers: were they really doing the work? Were they gossiping about the others in a little clique? After the first break of the afternoon, as the smokers came back in, there was tension in the air: they were a bit late, and I sensed we were seconds away from some kind of confrontation or destructive irritability.

At that point, the trainer made an extremely skilful intervention. He wanted to introduce the skill of reframing as a creative thinking tool ('reframing' is described in Box 9: it is a very useful skill to have up your sleeve in conflict management generally, and we shall refer to it again later in this chapter). So he decided to ask the group to reframe this problem in as many positive ways as it could:

> The split between smokers and non-smokers in the group means the group spends less time together as a whole and learning opportunities are lost.

Box 9

INTRODUCTION TO REFRAMING

An old Chinese Taoist story describes a farmer in a poor country village. He was considered very well-to-do because he owned a horse that he used for ploughing, for riding around, and for carrying things. One day his horse ran away. All his neighbours exclaimed how terrible this was, but the farmer simply said, 'Maybe.'

A few days later the horse returned and brought two wild horses with it. The neighbours all rejoiced at his good fortune, but the farmer just said, 'Maybe.'

The next day the farmer's son tried to ride one of the wild horses; the horse threw him and broke the boy's leg. The neighbours all offered their sympathy for this misfortune, but the farmer again said, 'Maybe.'

The next week conscription officers came to the village to take young men for the army. They rejected the farmer's son because of his broken leg. When the neighbours told him how lucky he was, the farmer replied, 'Maybe.'

_____

The meaning that any event has depends upon the 'frame' in which we perceive it. When we change the frame, we change the meaning. Having two wild horses is a good thing until it is seen in the context of the son's broken leg. The broken leg seems to be bad in the context of peaceful village life; but in the context of conscription and war, it suddenly becomes good.

This is called *reframing*: changing the frame in which a person perceives events in order to change the meaning. When the meaning changes, the person's responses and behaviours also change.

The more reframing you can do, the more choices you have.

Bandler and Grinder (1982)

He introduced this 'problem' with humour, and also made it absolutely clear that this apparently negative state of affairs could certainly be reframed as something positive. So he made sure the smokers did not feel that it was a covert attack on them. In fact, they expressed immediate relief that the issue had been brought to the surface.

The energy level in the room shot up, and people started coming up with all sorts of new ways of looking at the problem, including these:

> The split between smokers and non-smokers gives everyone an opportunity to learn to control their paranoia.

> The split... gives everyone an opportunity to demonstrate tolerance.

As an exercise in the power of reframing it worked well; and as a way of redirecting potentially negative energy towards learning it worked superbly. People were really engaged, because the topic was something they felt strongly about; and they are unlikely to forget the technique of reframing!

When it is not working

I once ran a programme on teamworking skills for a small organisation that had been through a recent round of redundancies. One of the key events of the programme was a visit by the MD, during which I facilitated a discussion between him and the participants on how teamworking in the organisation could be improved. The discussion went well, in that people said some of what was on their minds and the MD managed to ask questions and to continue to try to understand people's viewpoints even when he was obviously tempted to become defensive. But I certainly had to keep a fairly tight control over the process.

It was in the evening during dinner that the conflict really started. Alcohol did not help, of course, but I was aware that all around me entrenched positions were being taken, feelings were running high, and that the MD was having a series of arguments, culminating in something that came perilously close to a shouting match with one individual.

These evening discussions were not constructive in any way. Exhausted, the MD returned to his office the following morning with no clearer understanding of his staff's points of view. Drained, the participants arrived for the first session of the next day feeling resentful, lethargic, and vaguely apprehensive.

The issues for us as trainers

Given the inevitability and – often – *desirability* of conflict, we have to explore the following issues as trainers:

- How can we encourage confrontation of difficult questions and the expression of different views without destructive personal conflict?
- How can we create an environment in which our participants handle conflict effectively?
- How can we use the energy that conflict generates to progress the learning agenda?
- How and when should we calm things down?

The importance of understanding our own reactions to conflict

It is clear from a range of psychological theories and research that conflict evokes strong responses in most of us. Physiological studies have described the strong chemical reactions that arise from being in conflict situations – leading to physical symptoms that we can all recognise: increased heart rate, flushing, 'tingling' in various parts of our body, fast breathing, and so on. Conflict is the evolutionary prelude to a physical fight and our body prepares itself accordingly. Psychoanalytical approaches propose that conflict in adult life reminds us forcefully of conflict with our parents, of disapproval, punishment, even rejection; it has the power to take us back to how we felt in childhood. Social psychology points out that conflict carries with it the threat of exclusion from the group. We saw in Chapter 5 what a powerful influence that threat exerts over our emotions and behaviour.

So perhaps the most important starting place for us as trainers in developing our ability to handle conflict is to understand our own reactions to it and acknowledge that we find it difficult. It almost certainly makes us anxious, and we need to develop ways of setting that anxiety to one side so that it does not inhibit our creativity and reduce our effectiveness.

Here is a sequence of questions that psychology suggests we should reflect on, to learn more about how and why we personally respond to conflict in the way we do:

- Think of a recent situation when you have been in direct conflict with someone else. At what point did you begin to have strong feelings? What were you thinking at that point? What were you feeling, physically? What did these thoughts and feelings lead you to do?

- What are your values in relation to conflict? Do you, for example, think that conflict between people is often necessary to get at the truth? Or do you think that peace should be kept at all costs? Do you think it is better to 'have things out in the open'? Or do you think that words said in the heat of the moment cause more damage than they are worth?

- What have been the outcomes of key conflicts in your life?

- Who generally 'wins' in the conflicts that you have?

- How was conflict expressed and handled in the family you were born into? What were your feelings as a child when conflicts occurred?

Few of us are neutral in relation to conflict. At two extremes, we may seek to avoid it at all costs or we may provoke it obsessively; both these reactions are signs of anxiety. But we need to *become* neutral in relation to conflict in our training room so that we can:

- observe and understand it
- keep it within 'safe' limits
- use its energy to promote learning.

Let us further explore insights from psychology into the nature and meaning of conflict, so that we can perhaps achieve this goal.

Insights from Freudian theory

Freud developed a complex theory of the human psyche on the basis of years of clinical work with patients, and his observations of everyday behaviour. Ferocious arguments still rage about whether Freud was a genius or a charlatan (he was probably both), about whether his theory contains fundamental truths or a bundle of psycho-babbling fictions, and about whether Freudian psychology has been a tremendous liberating influence for twentieth-century man or a repressive and pessimistic prison. At any event, you cannot claim to have explored psychology fully unless you have explored Freud; and his theory and some of the simpler approaches that the full-blown theory has spawned have a lot to say on the subject of conflict.

Id, ego, super-ego

Freud proposed that there are three parts to the human psyche: the id, the ego, and the super-ego. The id comprises our instincts and biological impulses – for food, sex, and so on. The ego manages the whole psyche in relation to the external world so that the individual survives, physically and psychologically. It includes functions such as memory, perception and learning, since it is directed towards external reality and towards adapting the individual to the demands of that external reality. The super-ego is sometimes called the 'conscience' of the psyche: it represents all the demands the individual has taken on board from authority figures (parents, society, religion).

Freud maintained that by far the most important element in the development of the super-ego is the parents. It is as if we each had our parents inside our head, telling us what to do and what not to do, challenging and judging our behaviour when the impulses of our id do not fit the accepted norms.

It is interesting to read some of Freud's own descriptions of the id, ego and super-ego to capture their flavour and distinctiveness.

- '[The id] is the dark, inaccessible part of our personality; what little we know of it we have learnt from our study of [dreams]... we call it a chaos, a cauldron full of seething excitations.'

- 'The ego represents what may be called reason and common sense... Thus in relation to the id it is like a man on horseback, who has to hold in check the superior strength of the horse...'

- '...the id and super-ego have one thing in common: they both represent the influences of the past – the id the influence of heredity, the super-ego the influence... of what is taken over from other people – whereas the ego is principally determined by the individual's own experience, that is by accidental and contemporary events.'

Strachey (1953–66)

Energy, conflict and anxiety

Freud believed that the id, ego, and super-ego are in constant conflict, and it is the way that conflict is resolved which determines the individual's personality. In particular, the strong instinctive needs of the id come into conflict with the super-ego's requirements; this conflict has to be resolved by the ego. (We cannot, for example, have sex with everyone we find attractive.) Until the conflict is resolved, there is anxiety.

In order to remove the anxiety, the mechanism that the

ego uses most is *repression*. In other words, the ego makes sure that unresolved conflict is buried at an unconscious level, and so it defends itself. These 'ego defences' are usually unconscious themselves, and are often perfectly healthy in the short term – it would probably not help any of us to be aware, for example, of a deep desire to kill a sibling. But because this is all under the surface, there is always the frightening possibility of something causing it to emerge. Again, sometimes the repressive defence mechanism stops us functioning in a healthy way, because we misinterpret reality, trying to avoid the insights about ourselves and the underlying conflict that it might set in train. So I might feel angry with a colleague in a workshop because she has 'stolen' an idea of mine; the anger is disproportionate because in fact, unbeknown to me, it has triggered repressed anger that I used to feel at my sister when she 'stole' my mother's affection; and so the conflict escalates destructively without either party knowing why.

This sort of thinking about the structure of the human psyche suggests that it is important but difficult to keep conflict within manageable bounds. Conflict is a sort of universal psychic trigger, reminding us of the hidden conflicts in our unconscious, and threatening to destabilise the control we have constructed to hold ourselves together.

Insights from transactional analysis

A Swiss psychotherapist, Eric Berne, developed a therapeutic approach called 'transactional analysis' which is founded loosely on Freud's idea of the id, ego, and super-ego. It is a particularly useful approach for conflict situations.

Parent, adult, child

Berne suggested that we should think of our psyche as having three parts: the parent part, the adult part, and the child part. The parent part is our internalisation of our parents (corresponding loosely to Freud's 'super-ego'). The adult part is our rational, mature self (corresponding loosely to the 'ego'). The child part is all our uninhibited desires and wishes (you will see the similarity to the 'id').

Berne's terms are easier to understand than Freud's – and they are also easier to relate to. Intuitively we know that sometimes we behave as if we were children again, sometimes we hear ourselves sounding 'just like our father', and at other times we are simply our grown-up selves. It makes sense to think of ourselves as having these three aspects to our psychological make-up.

At any time, in any 'transaction' with someone else (for 'transaction', we can read 'interaction'), we are operating from one of these three parts. Here are some examples. Suppose I say to you: 'What a nice day it is today!' Your 'adult' might respond, 'Yes, isn't it..? I wonder how long this good weather will last.' Your 'parent' might respond, 'And about time too – this dull weather has been bad for all of us!' Your 'child' might respond, 'Let's take the afternoon off and go out for walk.'

The 'adult' part is associated with calm rationality. The 'parent' part can be either 'critical' (making judgements, telling others what they should and should not do, giving advice), or 'nurturing' (caring, looking after others). The 'child' part can be either 'adapted' (obedient or disobedient but basically responding to 'parental' rules), or 'free' (playful, creative, uninhibited).

In any interaction between two people (a 'transaction' in Berne's terminology), each individual will be operating from one of his three parts, and addressing one of the other party's parts. Figure 4 on page 124 represents diagrammatically a transaction in which her 'parent' addresses his 'child' and his 'child' replies to her 'child'.

Figure 4

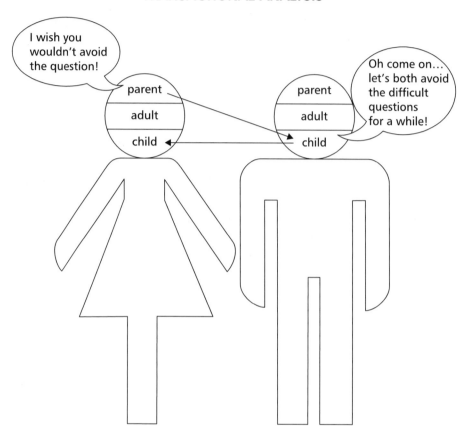

TRANSACTIONAL ANALYSIS

When conflict occurs, people will typically get locked in critical parent to critical parent transactions like this one.

A: 'You shouldn't criticise management: they're doing their best.'

B: 'Personally, I resent the way you always defend them.'

A: 'In fact, you're just far too quick to blame.'

B: 'Hark who's talking! You appear to be blaming *me* for the direction this conversation's taking!'

Or critical parent to adapted child transactions like this one.

A: 'It's time you all came back to the main room now.'

B: 'We're just finishing our coffee, *miss!*'

A: 'Well, I'm trying to keep to the timetable, as you asked me to – I'd appreciate some co-operation.'

B: 'We'll come when *we're* ready.'

'Hooking the adult': a way out of conflict

Berne's study of transactions suggests that if the two parties persist in parent/parent or parent/child interactions, conflict is likely to escalate. But one person can get the transaction out of conflict and into constructive dialogue if they force themselves to operate from their adult part and break the sequence.

Remember that the adult part is rational, information-giving and information-seeking. It is often an effort to move out of the instinctive emotional response into a rational one; but by asking a fact-seeking question, or offering a neutrally stated fact, we can do it.

Let us imagine how this could change the two 'transactions' we have just considered.

A: 'You shouldn't criticise management: they're doing their best.'

B: 'Personally, I resent the way you always defend them.'

A: 'In fact, you're far too quick to blame.'

B – Adult: 'You may have a point. Tell me what you've seen that makes you think they're trying.'

———————

A: 'It's time you all came back to the main room now.'

B: 'We're just finishing our coffee, *miss!*'

A – Adult: 'How much longer do you think you'll be? I need to adjust the timings for this afternoon.'

B – Adult: 'No more than five minutes.'

———————

In the second example, the adult response elicited a further adult response from the other party, and the potentially destructive pattern was defused.

As trainers, we need to work hard at staying 'adult' and at 'hooking the adult' in our participants. Although it is difficult not to 'snap back' emotionally when challenged, if we can stay curious and exploratory, trying to get as much information as we can about what is going on, we shall avert pointless conflict, and ultimately make our own lives much less stressful.

Life positions

Berne's transactional model can be extended to describe four different attitudes to our general relationships with others, or what are sometimes called four different 'life positions'.

Figure 5 illustrates these diagrammatically.

Figure 5

THE FOUR LIFE POSITIONS

I'm OK, You're OK	I'm OK, You're not OK
I'm not OK, You're OK	I'm not OK, You're not OK

If two people are operating from their adult parts, they are in the 'I'm OK, you're OK' box. They are comfortable with themselves, and with the other person; they are interacting as equals. Conflict tends to occur in the other three boxes – inappropriate aggression in 'I'm OK, you're not OK', inappropriate submission in 'I'm not OK, you're

OK' and inappropriate cynical manipulation in 'I'm not OK, you're not OK'.

As trainers, we have the responsibility to keep ourselves and our participants in the 'I'm OK, you're OK' box for as much of the time as possible. That is the box in which most learning occurs. Defences are thrown up in the other three boxes, for in each of those the self-esteem of one or both of the parties is being threatened. Since we have to protect our self-esteem or risk damage to our ego, in those boxes our energy is diverted away from learning towards protecting ourselves.

We shall know if and when we as trainers are not feeling OK. For most of us, there is some typical physical feeling. It happens when we are unsure of our material, uncomfortable with a relationship with someone in the group, overtired, distracted by stresses outside the training room, and so on. If we are not OK, we need to become OK, and if we need to take a break to do so, then that is what we should do. Only when we are feeling OK will we be good at handling conflict.

We need to learn the signs that one or more of our participants is not OK. It is safe to assume that when people behave defensively or aggressively, it is because they are not feeling OK. The most effective way to move them on is often by helping them to feel OK. Useful interventions to achieve this include:

- giving them a task that they will enjoy and do well
- reviewing the programme so far, giving everyone an opportunity to express their feelings
- affirming them in some way (by referring to a point they made earlier, by asking them for some specific help or information, by asking them to do something for each other).

One of the keys to encouraging confrontation while avoiding destructive conflict is keeping people in the 'I'm OK, you're OK' box. It needs to be a constant preoccupation of the trainer. If she does it well, her efforts will be invisible, but like the swan's powerful leg strokes underwater it will be these efforts that propel the group forward, rather than allowing it to get stuck.

Insights from neurolinguistic programming (NLP)

We introduced NLP in Chapter 2 and have referred to it a number of times since. As it focuses on the psychology of excellent communication, it is not surprising that it contains some useful approaches to handling conflict; we shall look at two of these.

Metamirror

When we think of people in conflict, we think of them as being stuck. Phrases such as 'locked in conflict' or 'beating my head against a brick wall' vividly evoke the way conflict forces people to take a position, and prevents their leaving it. The 'metamirror' is an NLP technique to release people from their positions.

Let me introduce it by asking you to use it on yourself.

Think of a relationship you currently have that is characterised by conflict. Call the person with whom you have this relationship into your mind. Concentrate on picturing them as they are when you are with them.

Place two chairs opposite each other, and sit on one of them. Imagine that the person you have called to mind is sitting on the chair opposite. Visualise that person. If you usually hear or sense anything in particular when they are present, call that to mind too. What are you feeling now? Concentrate on experiencing exactly what you experience when you are with this other person.

Now change chairs, and become that other person. See yourself in the chair opposite as they see you. Hear yourself as they hear you. Sense yourself as they sense you. What are you feeling now, as them? What are you thinking?

Concentrate on being them, in this difficult relationship with you.

Now stand up, move away from the chairs a little, and look at both you and the other person as if you were a detached external observer. What do you see? You have insights from being inside both these people. Is there any advice you would give to yourself? Stay in that position for a while, observing and thinking carefully about these two people, and what goes on between them.

When you feel ready, return to your own chair. Now you are back there, with the insights you have gained from the other positions you have visited, what will you do differently next time you meet this person with whom you have had so much conflict? Plan it in some detail. (You can continue the metamirror by visiting the other positions and imagining what the other person will see and feel when you do those different things.)

That is the end of the metamirror exercise.

This is a good exercise to do when you feel conflict between yourself and some or all of the group. It helps you 'hook your own adult part', because it is about being curious, exploring, and getting more information. It is also a good exercise to get participants to do, if the subject matter of the course lends itself (most interpersonal and communications skills training will do so). If you include it early on, participants will have it in their repertoire for managing any difficulties that occur between them during the course.

Reframing

Do you remember reframing from earlier in this chapter (page 116)? It is a great way of escaping from 'stuck' positions, as we saw.

If you find your own attitude to a participant getting 'stuck' – for example, in the perception that he is 'difficult' – you should practise re-framing his 'difficult' behaviour:

- He has a lot of integrity, and will not ever pretend to agree.
- He is looking after the rest of the group.
- He is taking a lonely position against you, so that the rest of the group can feel warm towards you.
- He respects your knowledge and competence greatly and so feels free to challenge you and get as much from you as he can.
- He is creating opportunities for you to develop your skill in reframing!

When you notice two or more participants sinking in an argument that is going nowhere, try to throw them a reframe as a life-belt. For example, imagine an argument about whether the 'scribe' in a brainstorming session should add his own ideas to the brainstorm. You can reframe this argument as a shared concern that brainstorming rules are made absolutely clear. Imagine an argument about whether car parking spaces should be allocated according to the seniority of the car owner (always a topic guaranteed to generate a lot of heat and little light). You can reframe the argument as a good exercise in presenting views forcefully, which will serve as a useful warm-up to the next session!

Reframing is one of the most effective skills to have for managing conflict, because it offers people escape routes that allow them to get out of conflict without suffering any damage to their self-esteem. Often they will retain the energy that the conflict generated, but use it more productively.

Insights from systems thinking

You may remember we came across systems thinking in Chapter 4, where we were talking about the power that systems (like the family or the workgroup) can exert either to keep an individual's behaviour the same, or encourage it to change.

The metamirror technique that we have just looked at is an example of systems thinking in action. By focusing not just on one person in an interaction (typically, the 'difficult' person) but on all the people in the transactional system, we understand more, and see more possibilities for change.

It is often helpful to see conflict as an inevitable result of the way a system is organised (for example, top management versus middle management, partners versus employees, unions versus bosses) rather than the *fault* of one or other party. Rearranging the system is often the best way to get rid of conflict.

Suppose your participants have separated into two 'camps'. Mix them up; or better still, design a task that depends for its success on co-operation between the two camps.

Look out for functional conflict: people taking opposite positions so that the different perspectives will be fully appreciated. Often individuals caught up in a conflict like this are actually doing it on behalf of the whole group. You can make this explicit; 'I think it's been particularly useful for all of us to hear this debate between Tom and Julia: it's clarified the issues.'

'The left-hand column'

Peter Senge is a researcher and practitioner in organisational learning. His approaches to teamworking and communication have widespread currency at the moment, and draw heavily on systems thinking.

One of the problems with conflict-laden conversations, Senge maintains, is that feelings remain unacknowledged, yet exert enormous influence over the course of the debate. One of Senge's ground rules for constructive communication is 'acknowledge and use your feelings'.

He proposes a technique to help people do just this, which he calls the 'left-hand column'. This is a good technique to get participants to use when they are discussing something contentious.

While the discussion is going on participants each make notes, in two columns. The right-hand column contains notes on what was actually said. The left-hand column contains notes of what the participants were thinking and feeling, but not saying. An example of an extract from such notes is shown below:

What I'm thinking and feeling	What is said
'Usual bull'	*Jim*: your point about training in the company is well made. We do not invest enough.
	Me: We need to estimate the real costs of this lack of investment.
'He's always making excuses for Jim!'	*Fred*: Mind you, there is not a lot of spare cash around at the moment.
'I'm so angry right now.'	*Jim*: You're right. Perhaps our cautious approach is justified.

At the end of the discussion, people look at their notes and ask themselves these questions:

- What has led me to think and feel this way?
- What was I trying to accomplish?
- Did I accomplish it?
- Why didn't I say what was in the left-hand column?
- What assumptions was I making about the others?
- What did it cost me, and the discussion, to operate this way? What were the benefits?
- What prevented me from acting differently?
- How could I use my left-hand column as a resource to improve our communications?

The group, once it has learned the technique, can use it to improve its communication about contentions issues. Individuals can stop the discussion and say – 'I don't think we're focusing on the real issue. Let me tell you what I've got in my left-hand column...'

The left-hand column approach acknowledges that feelings can run high, and gives people a way of managing them.

In brief

- The training room is an environment where clashes between people, and between views, often occur. As trainers, we need first to be able to face such clashes calmly, second to provide ways out of them and third to turn the energy they generate to positive purposes.

- The areas of psychology we turned to for insights in this chapter are Freudian theory, transactional analysis, neurolinguistic programming and systems thinking.

- Freudian theory draws our attention to the universality of conflict, and to its power to trigger deep anxieties in each of us – trainer and participants alike.

- Transactional analysis suggests we should:
  - ☐ elicit the rational, exploratory part of our participants at times of conflict by being rational and exploratory ourselves
  - ☐ work hard to keep ourselves and our participants in a state of mind where self-esteem is high, and we feel comfortable and equal in our relationships with others
  - ☐ always remember to look for signs that someone's self-esteem has been damaged when he appears aggressive or confrontational.

- Neurolinguistic programming suggests we should:
  - ☐ use a practical technique for putting ourselves in someone else's shoes at times of conflict, and teach this technique to our participants
  - ☐ practise the art of 'reframing', of understanding conflicts and impasses differently, in order to help our participants find a way out of both.

- Systems thinking suggests we should:
  - ☐ avoid blaming an individual for 'causing' conflict

□   give people a practical technique for acknowledging and using their feelings of frustration and hostility, rather than succumbing to them.

8

Facilitating Transfer of Learning

All trainers are preoccupied at times with that 64,000-dollar question: does training really make a difference? We are expected to provide, as well as the training itself, a plan for evaluating the training's effectiveness. We are beset on all sides by cynics – or perhaps realists – who tell us we are wasting our time. I recently did a training needs analysis for a firm of land agents; one of the primary needs identified was 'training in management skills for the partner'. In fact various courses had already been run – on appraisal skills, on delegation, on motivating staff; the junior staff commented that 'Partners try a bit harder after the course, but it wears off after a few weeks'. This is the kind of comment that makes us question whether anything we do in the training room transfers, solidly and permanently, to the workplace.

Yet there is also plenty of evidence that training *can* make a difference. A recent review of research into interpersonal skills training by Oxford psychologist Michael Argyle concluded that such training is effective for a wide range of work skills (Mackintosh and Colman 1994). He cites one piece of research, for example, that showed that training for managers, supervisors and leaders of all kinds resulted in increased productivity and sales for the company, and raised job satisfaction and reduced absenteeism among their staff. Music to a trainer's ears!

In this chapter we shall look at what psychology can tell us about how to help people learn in the training environment in a way that transfers to the environments in which they work. We have already looked at the vital factor of eliciting their commitment to change, in Chapter 4. (As one psychologist has put it, training cannot work if people do not.) In this chapter we shall be looking at the mechanisms of learning as psychologists have described them, to see what kinds of learning stick and under what kinds of circumstances.

When it works

I was once a participant with a team on an effective meetings course. Up until that course our meetings had been something of a shambles, characterised by lengthy argument leading to action plans that were never completed. The team was full of strong personalities. One of the things we were particularly bad at was delegating a piece of creative and/or important work to one member, contributing supportively, but then basically letting them get on with it. We were always meddling in, and sniping at, each other's work on behalf of the team.

The trainer running our course had some fairly standard points to make about effective meetings. But what she did which really transformed our meeting was to design with us, there and then, a unique meetings process that fitted our subject matter and our decision-making approach. We called the process an 'alignment session', and it was based on Senge's principles of skilful discussion (Senge 1994).

After the training we used this new meetings process whenever we needed to support and review each other's work. We found it shortened our meetings, led us to plan actions which we did carry out afterwards and also, most importantly, made our meetings enjoyable. We were still using it a year after the training.

Some of the characteristics of this learning that transferred so effectively to the workplace you will recognise in the psychological theories and models of learning that we shall look at shortly. These characteristics included:

- subject matter of high and immediate relevance to the learners
- readiness on the part of the participants to learn something of this kind
- learning under similar conditions to those at the workplace (in the team, discussing typical work issues)
- trying things out.

When it is not working

One of the most dispiriting experiences I have had as a trainer concerned the delivery of a five-day consultancy skills programme to the human resource team of a high street bank. The programme itself went well, and, as had been intended, the team learned a lot about working together, as well as about how to do effective internal consultancy.

About three weeks after the programme, the bank announced a sudden and massive reorganisation. The team I had worked with was completely disbanded. The concept of internal consultancy by human resource people was shelved. With no opportunity to practise their newly acquired skills, I am sure my participants soon forgot them.

I often reflect on this experience as a potent illustration of the fact that whatever we may do in the training room to facilitate transfer of learning, it is events outside it that often determine whether our efforts will be successful (and see Chapter 4, 'Insights from systems thinking', pages 63 to 67).

The issues for us as trainers

In trying to design and deliver training that promotes lasting learning for our participants, we need to know more about:

- how learning occurs: what helps it and what hinders it

- what makes learning 'fade' over time, and what can be done to make it last

- whether certain kinds of learning are more likely to transfer from the training room to the workplace, and what those kinds of learning are.

Insights from classical 'learning theory'

Perhaps the most surprising thing about classical learning theory is that it was developed mostly on the basis of research using rats and pigeons – species that, I'm sure we would all agree, learn a great deal less than us humans! The psychologists who were responsible for this work wanted to construct a theory of learning that was based only on what could be observed. In other words, people talking about what was going on inside their heads was of no interest at all to these researchers. They wanted psychology to be truly scientific, so any form of research that involved introspection or subjective data was off limits. They chose to work with animals because they reasoned that in that way they could discover the basic building blocks of learning – by controlling and studying changes in animal behaviour in ways that would be neither possible nor permissible with humans.

So classical learning theory is a fairly extreme – and some would say restricted – psychological field. We should pay it some attention, however, for these three reasons:

- The theory it gave rise to has had, in its own way, as much influence as Freud's theory of the unconscious mind.

- It contains some important, if rather basic, insights into the fundamental mechanics of learning.

- Other more sophisticated psychological approaches to learning have been derived from it, or developed in reaction against it.

The power of association

The American psychologist John B Watson believed that a science of psychology had to confine itself to two sets of observable data: what is done to the subject (*stimuli*); and what the subject does (*responses*). Perhaps the most famous psychology experiment of all time was that conducted by Russian scientist Ivan Pavlov in order to investigate the relationship between stimuli and responses (see Box 10).

Box 10

PAVLOV'S CLASSICAL CONDITIONING EXPERIMENT

A dog was held as still as possible in a specially constructed harness. The dog had never before been exposed to the sound of a bell, and Pavlov (the experimenter) observed that the dog did not salivate when a bell was rung. So he called the bell a 'neutral stimulus'. He then rang the bell and immediately afterwards gave food to the dog. He repeated this pairing of food and bell a number of times. Each time, the dog salivated. Then Pavlov rang the bell on its own (with no food). The dog salivated to the sound of the bell alone. So the bell had become a 'conditioned stimulus' for salivation, because it had been paired with a natural, that is to say 'unconditioned', stimulus – food.

Watson decided that Pavlov's experiment held the key to understanding learning, and that all learning, including human learning, could be described as sequences of conditioned responses. In Watson's view, as one thing becomes associated with another, we learn to respond to it in new ways – that is, our behaviour changes as a result of experience. Our brains are an ever-developing mass of stimulus-response connections, with 'learning by association' essentially explaining all learning. When I learn to speak, I am doing so because certain sounds are associated with certain objects or events. When I learn to read, I am doing so because certain symbols on a page are associated with certain sounds. And so on.

Another American psychologist, Edward L Thorndike, agreed with Watson and took the theory further, with experiments on cats in 'puzzle boxes'. A hungry cat was put in a box. The cat had to manipulate a latch on the door of the box. At first when the cat was placed in the box, it would struggle and meow. At some point it would accidentally do the right thing to the latch, release the door of the box, and get out to the food. The cat would then be put back in the box for another attempt. Thorndike found that the cat became gradually quicker at getting out of the box. He explained this by saying an association was being formed, and gradually strengthened, between a certain movement on the part of the cat (response) and access to food (stimulus). He called this kind of conditioning 'instrumental' because the cat was learning a response that was instrumental in getting to the food it wanted. He called the training process in which the cat had to manipulate the latch repeatedly to get the food a process of 'reinforcement', because this process was reinforcing the association between the cat's movement and the food.

I think it is interesting to discover the painstaking experiments that are the origins of words we now use loosely and without thinking in the training context: 'association', 'reinforcing', sometimes even 'conditioning'.

Rewards and punishments

The next major development in classical learning theory was brought about by B F Skinner, one of the most famous names in the whole of psychology. Not only did he develop an extremely elegant, well thought-out theory of all learning; he went on to build a whole life philosophy and political orientation. His ideas gave rise to a new educational approach, to new types of therapy for mentally disturbed people, to new thinking on how criminals should be dealt with, and even to a vision of a Utopian society.

Skinner's experiments were carried out on rats and pigeons. Rats had to press levers in boxes to get food pellets; pigeons had to peck at keys. Skinner and his associates could arrange all sorts of contingencies around the animal's response and the delivery of food. For example, in one experiment pigeons got food if they pecked at a key when a certain tone was played, but not if a different tone was played. They learned to peck at the key only when the 'rewarding' tone was played.

Food is a 'positive' reinforcer, because it makes it more likely that the response associated with it will occur. Skinner and his associates also experimented with 'negative' reinforcers, such as electric shocks, which make it less likely that the associated response will occur.

Skinner and his associates discovered that all sorts of learning could be achieved simply by arranging appropriate contingencies of rewards and punishments – positive and negative reinforcers. They found that reinforcement still worked – in fact, often worked better – even when it did not occur on every occasion. So a pigeon getting a food pellet on average only 30 per cent of the times it pecked the key would still learn to peck that key vigorously.

No one now doubts the power of association, nor the effectiveness of rewards and punishments, in the learning process. From the relatively benign 'star charts' of the primary school to the indisputably wicked electric shocks of the brainwasher, the theory and practice of the 'conditioning' approach to learning have become part of our everyday thinking.

As trainers, we are often unsure what to do about rewards and punishments. We do not like the sense of manipulation engendered by a conscious use of them. We feel that we should be dealing with our participants as colleagues and equals, not arranging a set of reinforcement contingencies around them as if they were laboratory rats; it feels disrespectful. We want to increase our participants' choice, not restrict it.

Yet learning theory, and all the psychological thinking that has developed since, reminds us that we will be wielding powerful rewards and punishments, whether we like it or not. The learning theory research into humans – rather than animals – demonstrates the amazing range of 'stimuli' that can be punishing or rewarding for people. They include:

- eye contact
- attention
- opportunity to be heard
- recognition of one's point of view
- inclusion in a particular group
- praise and 'positive strokes' that slip from every trainer without her even noticing it... 'I agree', 'That's an interesting point', 'Well put'....

These are just some of the more obvious positive reinforcers that we will inevitably be using in the training room, like it or not. Again, working with people as opposed to animals has shown that almost anything can be either a positive or negative reinforcer, depending on an individual's past experience, his values, his 'mental map'. The extravert will experience opportunities to make presentations as a reward; the shy participant will experience those same opportunities as a punishment.

I think that learning theory encourages us as trainers to do two things. The first is to be aware of, and disciplined in, our use of reinforcement contingencies. The second is to give away to the group our power as reinforcers as much as we can. Let me give you a concrete example.

I often run team development programmes. One of the most useful ways I can help a team to learn new and lasting constructive patterns of communicating with each other is by suggesting to them a set of communications 'ground rules' which I can enforce on their behalf. I ask them if the ground rules adequately describe how they would like to operate (typical ground rules would be – 'assume positive intent', 'explore and understand points of difference', 'clarify ambiguous terms at all times'); I ask them to amend or add to the ground rules; and then I make an explicit contract with the team that I will reward communication that is in line with those rules, and punish communication which is not ('rewards' and 'punishments' are usually administered in review sessions following periods of communication).

If we model disciplined use of reinforcement contingencies, and give the power of determining those contingencies to the participants by being explicit about them, then we can use constructively one of the most powerful mechanisms for establishing lasting learning. We can also suggest ways in which participants can set up similarly constructive reinforcement contingencies back in the workplace. Teams, for example, will often choose to appoint an 'observer' at meetings who will review the meeting at the end according to the ground rules they have been applying during training.

Learning theory suggests that we are fooling ourselves if we think we can operate neutrally as trainers, without rewarding and punishing. People are too subtle; but we can operate responsibly.

Insights from cognitive approaches

Whereas classical learning theory emphasises stimuli and responses – the observable data about learning – cognitive approaches attempt to deal with what is going on inside our heads – mental models, organising structure, patterns and so on. Much of the relevant research has been conducted under the heading of 'long-term memory research'.

As we have found when we have looked at psychology that attempts to describe the most complex aspects of human behaviour, the experiments are ingenious but the flexibility of the human mind refuses to be contained within their perfect constraints. None the less, there are pointers, suggestions and indicators that are of insight for us as trainers.

Unlimited capacity, faulty retrieval systems

You may remember from Chapter 3 that there is clear evidence that our capacity to attend, perceive and record in short-term memory is strictly limited. There is simply only so much information we can deal with at a time.

But when it comes to how much we can store, there appear to be no practical limits. An educated person remembers between 40,000 and 60,000 words. Elderly people can remember details of events that occurred 70 years ago. You may see a face in a crowd and recognise someone you have not seen for decades.

The problem is not that we cannot fit all the information in. It is that we cannot find it once it is in there. If you imagine our long-term memory as a library, once we put a book in it stays there. (The evidence for this includes the results of treatment of people with brain damage, where administering electric currents to different parts of the brain causes them to 'remember' events and facts of which they had previously had no conscious knowledge. Such findings suggest a wealth of 'hidden' information in our minds.)

The importance of organisation

You may remember from Chapter 3 that the single most important factor in how people deal with information is the meaning they attach to it. This applies just as much to information in long-term memory as it does to information that we are in the process of receiving.

We do not store information away passively. In that sense, our minds are not like libraries. We actively restructure the information we are storing, so that its relationship to other 'books on the shelf' near it is emphasised.

It was a British psychologist, Sir Frederick Bartlett, who did the first systematic work on how we organise meaningful material in our memories. He gave people stories to study. After 15 minutes, he asked them to write down as accurate a recollection of it as they could manage. He tested the subjects' memory of the story several times in the years that followed, and found they made a typical set of errors. These were as follows:

- People omitted details, particularly details that did not fit or seem important to their understanding of the story.

- They adapted the story so that it made more sense to them; they made it more logical.

- They chose some aspect of the story as the central theme, and made it more dominant in the way they retold the story.

- They distorted the material according to their own attitudes, reactions and feelings. For example, they might refer to a 'ghost' as 'a weird thing', or a 'black rider' as an 'ominous rider'.

Based on the results of these experiments, and many others involving all sorts of different material, Bartlett argued that one of the most important determinants of what is remembered is what he called 'effort after meaning'. He meant by this that when we commit something to memory, we reconstruct the information so that it makes more sense, and fits and associates with what we already know and understand. We try hard to make it mean a lot to us.

If we extrapolate from this to the training context, we conclude that to promote lasting learning, we need to make sure that people can fit their new skills and understanding into their existing reality. This is one of the reasons that training courses typically give people plenty of time to discuss new approaches and ideas. Through the process of discussion, people are transforming what the training is offering into something which makes sense for them.

We can see that understanding *why* we are learning something is of paramount importance. If the learning seems arbitrary, or worse still, out of line with our beliefs and values, we will discard it.

Context-specific learning

A not unrelated point is that memory for something tends to be best when we are in the same situation where we learned about that thing – or as close to it as possible. That is why the police set up expensive reconstructions of crimes when witnesses are few and far between. Being propelled back into the context of the crime by seeing it replayed will help some people remember things they did not know they knew.

One experiment showed that when people were taught aspects of scuba diving while under water, they remembered what they had been taught better when they were under water than when they were sitting by the pool. The reverse was also true: people who had been taught sitting by the pool remembered better there than under water.

All this suggests that the whole activity of training is fundamentally flawed, because the training room is so different from the work environment. Naturally, I do not personally hold that view; I just think that the psychology of context-specific learning draws to our attention that there is a significant gulf we have to help our participants cross. We do it by bringing the workplace into the training room, so far as we can, with case studies, role plays, discussions with actual work colleagues, planning for how things will be different when they go back to work, and so on.

Hierarchy of learning

It is clear from the variety of different psychological approaches to the study of learning that there are many different types of learning. Different schools of thinking focus on different types: although they might all like to claim they can cover all learning, in practice they will have selected just some aspects. Very simple associative learning is focused on by classical learning theory, for example; language learning by another set of theorists; and cognitivists focus on everyday human learning.

Benjamin Bloom developed a taxonomy of learning that attempts to describe different types of learning as a sequence of stages. Learning does not have to move through all these stages; perfectly adequate learning can occur at 'lower' levels; but the learning that will really be incorporated into living is the learning that has moved right through the hierarchy. Figure 6 summarises Bloom's taxonomy.

Figure 6

BLOOM'S HIERARCHICAL LEARNING TAXONOMY

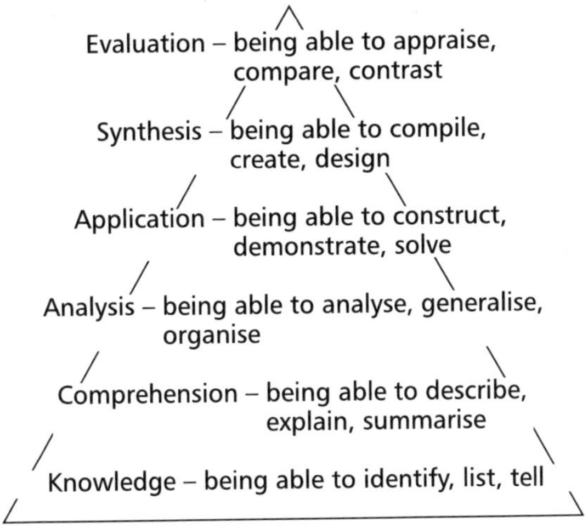

Evaluation – being able to appraise, compare, contrast

Synthesis – being able to compile, create, design

Application – being able to construct, demonstrate, solve

Analysis – being able to analyse, generalise, organise

Comprehension – being able to describe, explain, summarise

Knowledge – being able to identify, list, tell

So on a presentation skills programme, for example, participants might start by being introduced to the basic rules of effective presentation (knowledge). They might then be asked to suggest why these rules apply (comprehension and analysis). Then they might be asked to deliver a presentation conforming to the rules (application). After which they might be asked to suggest some new rules (synthesis). Finally, they might be asked to appraise each other's presentations (evaluation). By incorporating all these stages, the chances of the learning being truly integrated into the learner's way of doing things are greatly increased.

There is an even simpler formulation of the stages of learning that is often used in a training context, based on the fact that people first learn the rules, then practise them with some effort, and only after that do they really incorporate the new skills into their behavioural repertoire. The formulation says people move through the following stages.

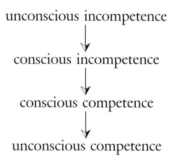

If we can enable participants to reach 'unconscious competence' on our programmes, then we can really have confidence the learning will stick.

Kolb's learning cycle

Another much-used – and useful – formulation of the different types and stages of learning is that of David A. Kolb. According to Kolb, any piece of successful learning will incorporate one or more of the following:

Doing: getting a baseline of understanding in a realistic setting

Reflecting: thinking about what you see and experience

Conceptualising: thinking about things logically, processing ideas internally and finding links and patterns

Experimenting: trying things out to see what happens.

The more we can include the whole range of learning activities on our training programmes, the more likely we are to promote lasting learning in all the participants. Kolb – and others since – argued that each of us has a preferred learning style. Some of us are active experimenters, others are reflective observers, still others inquisitive conceptualisers, and so on.

Kolb's different types of learning can be represented as a cycle. For truly integrated learning you can argue that the whole cycle needs to be completed at least once (see Figure 7).

Figure 7

KOLB'S LEARNING CYCLE

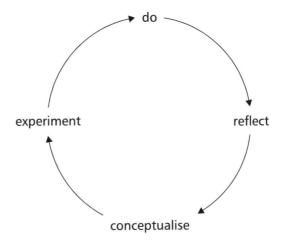

Insights from research into behaviour at work

For much of this chapter we have been looking at psychological research about learning under conditions very different from those of the training room: rats in boxes, people remembering stories, and so on. But there is a body of research into industrial psychology that is also of some relevance here, where changes for the better in the ways people do things at work have been studied directly.

These studies have indicated the following factors increase the likelihood that change will occur and last:

■ *knowledge of results*: if people are given information on how well they are doing, not only will they improve but they will work for longer without becoming tired

■ *attention from the organisation*: in a classic experiment, factory workers were given all sorts of incentives and improved conditions, to see which most improved their performance; nothing had a greater level of impact than simply participating in the experiment; in other words, if attention was paid to the workers, they improved their performance (the 'Hawthorne effect').

In brief

■ What is achieved in the training room has to cross a wide gulf before it can be said to be of any real value: the gulf between the training room and the workplace. Trainers need to address the bridging of that gulf.

■ Psychology has much to say about the nature of, and conditions for, permanent learning. In this chapter we looked at classical learning theory, cognitive approaches and research into behaviour at work.

■ Classical learning theory suggests that we should:

☐ never underestimate the power of association, and of rewards and punishments, to establish new patterns of behaving

- understand that for human beings the range of things that can act as rewards or punishments is immense: including eye contact or its withdrawal, specific affirmation of someone's point of view or the reverse, the opportunity to join or be excluded from particular groups
- give away to the group as far as we can our power as trainers to determine reinforcement contingencies (associations between certain behaviours and certain rewards and/or punishments)
- be self-aware, responsible and disciplined in our use of reinforcement contingencies.

■ Cognitive approaches suggest that we should:
- always give our participants as much time and opportunity as possible to 'make sense' of what they learn – by discussion, by trying things out, by reflecting
- make the learning environment as much like the working environment as possible
- give our participants opportunities to learn at a wide range of levels.

■ Research into behaviour at work emphasises the importance of knowledge of results and attention from the organisation in promoting lasting change.

9

Surviving as a Trainer

In this chapter I want to explore what psychology has to tell us about stress and its effective management. Is this because I think training is a particularly stressful occupation? Yes and no – a typical psychologist's answer!

In some ways training is a relatively stress-free occupation. A boss of mine once said to me: 'The great thing about training is it's *clean*. You go in, deliver a programme, and then it is done. You have a sense of completion, of closure.' Unlike general management, for example, there is not the volume of never-ending tasks, of things at the bottom of the in-tray that have been lurking for months, of messy and essentially unresolvable long-running interpersonal situations. All the research suggests that chronic stress – caused by anxieties and worries that gnaw away at us and become part of our lives – is much more damaging to our physical and emotional health than acute stress – the nerves we may have before a training programme, the rush of adrenaline as we are managing a difficult group – the sudden but clearly finite anxieties.

Again, in training we are more in control of what happens while we are delivering a programme than people are in many other kinds of work. Not only that, we generally get a lot of feedback on how we are doing, and plenty of recognition from our participants when things are going well. Jobs are much more stressful where we are not in control of how things ultimately turn out, where there is little feedback, or where recognition appears to bear little or no relation to our achievements and efforts.

Finally, training is essentially a hopeful activity. We are in the business of helping people realise more of what they can be, we are working for the most part with resourceful people, and often we and they achieve the goal. Unlike psychiatrists and therapists, we are not trying to bring about change in people who are at the end of their resources, for many of whom the prospect of change is remote or unrealistic.

So for all the above reasons, I think training is an activity that can nourish us. None the less, I believe we need to be aware of the stressful sides to it. In training, as we have seen over and again in this book, we are using ourselves – our whole selves – to achieve the objectives. Whether we are controlling our own emotional reactions to stay creative at times of conflict (Chapter 7), managing our inclination to join the group (Chapter 5), making sure we use reinforcers such as eye contact, praise and agreement thoughtfully rather than carelessly (Chapter 8), or doing any one of a thousand other things that make the difference between good and bad training, we are requiring a lot of ourselves at all levels. We are certainly requiring much in terms of emotional maturity and resilience. We need to be very 'fit' emotionally to do this well, and we need to check that we are not becoming unduly drained. (We also need to be physically fit, because delivering a training programme requires a lot of stamina, and of course stress has immediate and strong effects on physical fitness.)

Also, while I would not wish to push this analogy too far, some aspects of training overlap with the 'helping professions'. In such work, the risk is that we get overinvolved and that some of our own deep-seated anxieties are triggered by what is going on. We need to recognise when this is happening and know how to cope with it.

Finally, some aspects of training overlap with the 'performing arts'. We are up there, literally or metaphorically, on stage. We have to entertain and enliven. So we experience the kinds of stress that go along with being on show: 'stage fright', anxiety about 'public speaking', fear that we will make fools of ourselves.

In this chapter, therefore, we shall look at what psychology says about the nature and origins of stress, and how best to respond to it. What we learn will, it is hoped, also give us another resource that our participants can draw on. Sometimes attending a training programme gives people the space to think about their own stress, and they may want to talk to us about it. We should not cross the boundary into stress counselling proper (see Chapter 6), but we may be able to set them on the right path.

When it works

I was talking to a trainer colleague of mine who I happen to know is experiencing a great deal of stress and upheaval in his personal life at the moment. Yet he has a heavy training delivery load in areas such as managing change, general management skills, and personal effectiveness – all intense, emotionally demanding programmes in organisations that are in many cases going through difficult times. I asked him how he coped.

He thought for a while, and then described a process he goes through mentally in the few hours running up to the start of a programme. He first focuses on various aspects of his personal life, thinks about each briefly, and puts them to one side. Then he thinks about the programme ahead, the participants, and what he will be doing. He imagines exactly how he will feel at the end of the programme if things have gone well, and creates for himself a compelling vision of that. (Interestingly, he goes through the reverse process as he travels home at the end of a programme, setting his experiences of the training consciously and deliberately to one side, and re-engaging with his personal life.)

This colleague finds that he is:

∎ invigorated by running a piece of training

∎ relaxed for the most part during training, and when he feels stressed he can work out what to do to become relaxed again

∎ emotionally resourceful during training, finding creative ways through participants' boredom, frustration, anger and cynicism when these occur.

When it is not working

We all know the signs in ourselves of stress that is getting out of control. Here are some of the typical ones.

∎ physical – flushes, sweating, stomach cramp, headache, fatigue

∎ emotional – feeling depressed, panicky, angry, frightened, irritable

∎ behavioural – repetitive activity, mistakes, poor problem-solving, low creativity, avoidance.

The issues for us as trainers

We need to know:

∎ why we feel stressed at different times

∎ what kind of stress is normal and what is a danger sign

∎ what we can do to manage stress in the short term

∎ how we can live our professional lives in the long term to minimise destructive stress.

Insights from the physiology of stress

You may remember that in Chapter 3 we commented on how little understood neurophysiology is, so the 'physiology of thinking' is really a closed book to us, apart from some very general principles.

In contrast, the physiology of stress has been researched to the point where it is quite well understood. It tells us some useful things about the nature and power of our stress responses.

Extensive physical changes

The thing that happens to trigger our chain of physiological response to stress is that we perceive something as a threat. It could be an oncoming car that swerves into our path, a sarcastic comment by a participant on one of our training courses, or a course evaluation form with low ratings... or just about anything else, for that matter. The perception of threat sends a signal along our nerve pathways to a structure in the lower part of our brain called the hypothalamus. This part is very sensitive to the effects of drugs and intense emotion, and is largely responsible for changes in appetite, weight, water-balance and mood. When it receives the stress signal, it produces a chemical message which is sent to the pituitary gland (in our neck) and to the adrenal glands (near our kidneys). The pituitary gland produces the adrenocorticotrophic hormone (ACTH) and a thyroid-stimulating hormone (TSH).

ACTH then travels to the adrenal glands, where it triggers the production of cortisol. This increases the level of sugar in the blood and speeds up our metabolic rate (faster breathing, higher pulse rate and so on).

Adrenaline and noradrenaline are also produced as a result of chemical reactions in the adrenal glands triggered directly by the original chemical message from the hypothalamus. These hormones produce the 'fight or flight response': they rev the body up for action, making a great deal of energy instantly available. Adrenaline also focuses concentration and helps to improve memory.

There is a feedback loop back to the pituitary gland which continues to control the intensity and duration of the stress response.

Short-term stress is functional; long-term stress is not

You can see from the above description that the immediate effect of our physiological response to stress is to increase our resourcefulness: not only can we literally fight harder or run away faster, but we can also think more quickly and focus more intensely. So as trainers we should welcome the energy surge that comes with acute stress. It gives us the possibility of responding agilely and creatively.

But if stress continues over long periods of time, the adrenal glands become exhausted through overwork and cease to operate efficiently. Not only that, but other systems in our bodies will be overworked too – rather like an engine that has been constantly run on high revs. That is of course why so many physical disorders can be associated with stress (see Table 4).

Table 4

SOME COMMON STRESS-RELATED ILLNESSES

Mouth ulcers	Impotence
High blood pressure	Pre-menstrual pain
Palpitations	Asthma
Migraine	Backache
Diarrhoea	Neckache
Constipation	Irritable bladder
Heartburn	Eczema

So it is fine to experience moments of anxiety during a training programme – and probably much more effective than total complacency would be. But sustained anxiety will exhaust us and, ultimately, make us ill.

Insights from psychoanalysis

In the sections above I included 'a sarcastic comment by a participant' in a list of 'threats', where another example was the threat of a serious car accident. You may have wondered in passing as you read that list why events like hearing a sarcastic comment constitute threats at all; they are hardly life-threatening. And we all chanted as children:

> Sticks and stones may break my bones, but words will never hurt me.

Surely, when compared with fire-fighting or deep-sea diving, training must be one of the least threatening occupations. Psychoanalytic theory helps us to appreciate the nature – and the reality – of the threats to which we as trainers are exposed.

Projection and transference

We introduced the concepts of projection and transference in Chapter 5 (see Box 7). They are powerful psychological defence mechanisms. Projection stops us having to face up to the often uncomfortable truth about our own emotions, desires and motives. Instead of acknowledging that we are angry, for example, we behave in a way that makes someone else angry with us. This enables the anger to be expressed, but someone else bears the responsibility of expressing it. We get off lightly; they usually feel 'dumped on'. Yet they will find it hard to resist the projection, because of the powerful way the process works. Let me illustrate this with a true story from a training environment.

A tutor was working with a group of very highly educated and culturally sophisticated senior managers. In the group was a woman who was feeling anxious about the status of her job, and who was also feeling that her particular area of expertise was being increasingly undervalued by the organisation. She began to criticise the tutor's language and style of delivery. She interrupted him repeatedly, accusing him of using jargon and of citing inappropriate examples from organisations totally different from hers and from areas of work that had nothing in common with hers. The tutor ended up feeling so anxious and so undervalued that he had to hand over the running of the session to his colleague. The course participant had successfully, albeit unconsciously, projected her own feelings of anxiety and inferiority onto him.

Transference is a similarly powerful process. It occurs when people treat the trainer *as if* she were 'the boss', 'their rival', 'their mother'. If she is not careful, she starts behaving as if she really is that other person.

Why are we as trainers particularly likely to be the target of these kinds of pressure? It is because we are in a position of power in relation to the group. Psychoanalytic theory proposes that when someone is in a position of power in relation to us, it triggers the recollection of that first power relationship of all: our relationship as children with our parents. At that point, all sorts of emotions start flying around, and are often defended against by the mechanisms of projection and transference.

It is for this reason that we are in a *threatening* environment. At its worst, it is a psychic cauldron, other people's anxieties and our own deep anxieties and repressed hopes seething around us. As we sense these threats to our psychological and emotional survival (for the experience of too much intense negative emotion is literally that), we find our stress response is elicited. And of course other people are very good at finding our Achilles' heel, emotionally, and playing on that. Sometimes it is as if the training room is a stress-test of our emotional resilience.

Insights from the treatment of neuroses

Where the response to stress is extreme and so disproportionate to the threat that it prevents an individual from living a sensible life, it is called a neurosis (see Chapter 6, Box 8). Neuroses take many forms, from panic attacks to phobias to obsessive-compulsive disorders (such as constant hand-washing).

Some of the treatments of neurosis give us useful insights into how we can manage our own stress.

Rational–emotive therapy

A New York psychotherapist, Albert Ellis, bases his treatments on the notion that inappropriate emotional reactions (including sustained and uncontrollable stress) result from inappropriate beliefs that people have about themselves and their relationship to the world. If you can get people to change these beliefs and bring them more into line with reality, then the strong emotional reaction will disappear.

An example of such an erroneous belief would be:

> I should be thoroughly competent, adequate, and achieving in all possible respects if I am to consider myself worthwhile.

People holding this belief will become extremely stressed when they make even a small mistake.

Other examples of the erroneous beliefs, or 'irrational ideas', can be found in Box 11. You might find it interesting to see whether you are suffering from any of them as a trainer. (I certainly think that many of us suffer needless stress caused by the irrational idea that we should be liked and respected by every participant on every training course!)

When we feel ourselves becoming stressed in the training situation, rational–emotive therapy suggests that we should take some time to ask ourselves what it is we fear

Box 11

SOME IRRATIONAL IDEAS ACCORDING TO ELLIS

Irrational idea no. 1
It is a dire necessity for an adult human being to be loved or approved of by virtually every significant person in his community.

Irrational idea no. 4
It is awful and catastrophic when things are not the way one would very much like them to be.

Irrational idea no. 6
If something is or may be dangerous or fearsome, one should be terribly concerned about it and keep dwelling on the possibility of its occurring.

Irrational idea no. 8
One should be dependent on others, and need someone stronger than oneself on whom to rely.

or regret. Sometimes when we do this we discover that we are expending emotional energy fearing or regretting something that is just part of the natural order of things. Sure, one of our participants is flicking ahead in the workbook: a programme cannot move at the right pace for all of the participants all of the time. Yes, two of the participants have skipped the afternoon session: we need to find out why and then take action, but there may be perfectly good reasons; just because someone skips a session it does not mean we are a failure as a trainer. Certainly that last remark from the group was barbed, but we cannot expect the atmosphere to be sweet every minute of the day: it is late, and they are tired.

Rational–emotive therapy is about giving ourselves a break: a break from having to produce the best of all possible training in the best of all possible worlds.

The behaviour therapies

Phobias are intense fear reactions provoked by specific – and usually harmless – things. We can probably all think of a whole range of them, so used are we to the concept: arachnophobia, claustrophobia, agoraphobia, xenophobia...

The interesting thing is that irrational fear is so widespread. Pause for a minute to think as a trainer about what your irrational fears are. I have a colleague who is terrified of tripping up (literally) in front of the group. Another trainer I know is terrified of 'drying up' (completely forgetting what to say). Yet another fears she will be overcome by the need to go to the toilet while training! (Interestingly, these fears are all associated with humiliation.)

There is an interesting technique used in behaviour therapy with extremely phobic people that we can use on ourselves to reduce our stress reactions. Box 12 opposite gives a general overview of behaviour therapy and also describes the specific technique in which I am interested here: desensitisation.

We can use desensitisation on ourselves. First we need to learn relaxation techniques (these are useful to have in our repertoire anyway). Then we need to find a quiet place and start to imagine the things of which we are frightened. It is best if we start by imagining events of which we are only a little frightened. So, for example, if our big fear is of losing control of the group (see Chapter 5), we could start by imagining that we walk into the room and they do not stop talking. If we have imagined it right, we will feel the physical symptoms that typify our stress reaction.

We need to continue imagining this situation but practise our relaxation techniques and also 'play the tape' of the situation to some kind of resolution.

For example, we might imagine standing at the front of the room for quite a long time (keeping ourselves relaxed throughout this imagining) until one by one the group

Box 12

INTRODUCTION TO BEHAVIOUR THERAPY

Behaviour therapy is derived from behaviourism (see Chapter 8).

▌ The central idea is that you can change people's behaviour directly by the way you arrange stimuli, punishments and rewards, and that you do not need to investigate, or get the person to understand, why they behave in the way they do. So behaviour therapy is often contrasted with 'insight-oriented' therapies. Its theoretical roots are in experimental psychology and in Skinner's behaviourism.

▌ *Desensitisation therapy* involves presenting a stimulus that typically arouses anxiety while keeping the individual relaxed so the vicious cycle of association of fear and panic with that stimulus is broken. The client learns relaxation techniques, which he or she practises with the support of the therapist throughout. The therapist introduces stimuli in a gradual progression, from those that would normally elicit only the mildest anxiety to, eventually, stimuli that can provoke a full panic attack. Desensitisation therapy works well with phobias and other anxiety-related problems. (The therapist does not have to present the *actual* stimuli: he or she can get the client to imagine a graded series of anxiety-provoking situations, while remaining deeply relaxed.)

▌ Other related forms of therapy involving manipulating the emotions that someone feels in relation to a stimulus are *flooding* and *aversion therapy*. In flooding, an individual is put in the most fearful situation imaginable and kept there until they are calm, so they learn through experience that that situation does not kill them. In aversion therapy, people are punished for responding in certain ways, so that they learn not to respond in that way any more. Aversion therapy has been used with sex offenders.

▌ *Operant conditioning (shaping)* borrows techniques from experimental studies (with rats and pigeons, for example). It creates an environment where the whole relationship between behaviour and subsequent punishments and rewards is very strictly controlled in order to increase the frequency of certain behaviours and reduce the frequency of others.

▌ Some mental hospitals have set up 'token economies', where patients are 'paid' with plastic tokens for certain kinds of behaviour (such as doing kitchen chores, making their own beds). These tokens can later be exchanged for special privileges. Token economies appear to bring about significant changes in behaviour.

▌ Operant conditioning is also used a great deal with children – it has been applied to bed-wetting, thumb-sucking, tantrums, aggressive and hyperactive behaviour, asthma attacks, and poor school performance.

falls silent. We can then move on to imagine a slightly more frightening scenario.

I have personally found this technique has helped me to reduce considerably the level of stress I experience when delivering training.

Insights from the psychology of individual differences

All psychologists who study stress and its effects on human beings (as opposed to its effects on animals) agree that there is huge variability between people in terms of their 'stress profile'; that is:

- what they experience as stressful
- how much stress they can take before their health suffers
- what kinds of physical and psychological response to stress they typically have.

Type A versus Type B

Probably the best-known framework for differentiating between individuals and their typical stress profiles is the theory of the 'two types'.

In the 1960s, American psychologists Friedman and Rosenman studied the relationship between personality and the likelihood of suffering coronary heart disease (a condition commonly associated with stress – see Table 4, page 157). They found that people with certain types of behaviour pattern were much more likely to suffer from heart disease. Such people came to be known as 'Type A', and had some or all of the following characteristics:

- excessive drive
- extreme competitiveness
- unrealistic urgency, great impatience
- inappropriate ambition
- reluctance to reflect on themselves
- a strong need to control.

'Type B' personalities, in contrast, were characterised by:

■ a relaxed, easy-going approach to life
■ focus on quality of life rather than quantity of output or achievement
■ low competitiveness
■ a tendency for self-reflection.

Since the early studies, an impressive body of research evidence has been gathered supporting the view that the Type A/Type B distinction represents an important difference between people, and that Type A behaviour is strongly associated with stress-related illness.

Studies like these may make us feel that we have little control over our own responses to stress. After all, we did not choose to be Type A or Type B. Trainers who recognise Type A characteristics in themselves in particular may wonder if there is anything they can do.

In fact, there is much that can be done. We can practise behaving more like Type B by using on ourselves some of the therapeutic techniques we looked at earlier in this chapter. Also, we can work hard at ensuring that we are exposed to as few as possible of the things we personally find particularly stressful.

Powerful sources of stress

These things will be determined by our past experience, our concept of ourselves, our values and so on. For example, one situation that invariably stresses one of my colleagues is where he can see a solution clearly, and presents it, but the group he is working with does not listen. He feels his tension mount as, in his view, precious time is wasted when, to him, the 'answer' is obvious. Other colleagues of mine are not stressed by this situation at all. They shrug their shoulders, comment to themselves that 'You can take a horse to the water but you cannot make it drink', and move on. They are stressed more by training large groups, or by having to run long whole-group sessions, or by running a new programme that they have never observed anyone else run. (My first colleague is not stressed by any of this in the least.)

So the most important thing for us to do is to get to know what the particular stressors for us as individuals are. Psychological research suggests the sorts of places we should look are:

- the nature and size of the job, how clearly it is defined, how much control we have over it (stress increases when the job is too big for us, when the objectives are unclear, when we do not have the resources we need to do it, and so on)
- our relationships with the people with whom we work
- the climate and structure of the organisation in which we work
- our security and prospects
- our home lives, and in particular the interface between home and work.

Once we have identified particular sources of stress for us, we can take practical steps to reduce or eliminate them. That is the best form of stress management of all. A young colleague of mine, who was just beginning her training career and had had a couple of experiences with 'difficult' groups, realised that the most stressful thing for her was being alone as a trainer. So she made sure that she increased the amount of co-tutoring she did for a while, became much less anxious, and she now trains happily on her own.

One of the advantages that we have as trainers in terms of managing our stress is that in the training room we have a great deal of control over how things are organised. If we find that managing a large group is stressful, we can make sure that most work is done in small groups. If we need some time to reflect, we can give people a task or a topic for them to reflect on. We need to use our opportunities to control the training environment in order to reduce the stress we experience, and so to increase our own resourcefulness; our participants can only benefit from that.

In brief

- There are many stressful aspects to training. We need to understand where stress comes from for us, when it is damaging, and how to manage it.
- The physiology of stress, psychoanalysis, the treatment of neuroses, and research into individual differences are areas of psychology that provide some relevant insights.
- The psychology of stress suggests that we need to minimise chronic stress, which will exert damaging and wide-ranging effects on our physical health; long-term unresolved anxieties are the worst.
- Psychoanalysis reminds us that we need to be alert to the particular stresses that intense work with other people inevitably exposes us to.
- Various treatments for neuroses suggest that we need to:
  - examine ourselves for unrealistic assumptions about how effective we need to be as trainers, and learn to talk ourselves into more realistic assumptions
  - use relaxation techniques and mental imagery to overcome irrational fears.
- The psychology of individual differences tells us that we need to understand our own stress profile, and to take as many practical steps as possible to eliminate those things that stress us most, and most chronically.

Conclusion

You will remember that we set out in this book to do three things – to understand some of psychology's influence on general training practice, to investigate how ideas from psychology could usefully influence our own training practice further, and to develop a 'psychological frame of mind'.

So we have rampaged through a considerable volume of psychological research and theory, like small children in a big, exciting toy-shop. We have tried out all sorts of things that caught our interest and our eye, but we have not spent long on any one subject.

For those of you who already have a background knowledge of psychology, I hope this whistle-stop tour has rekindled your enthusiasm for exploring the links between psychology and training. For those of you who have read this book as an introduction to those links, I hope you will read more, and in more depth, about psychology. Whenever I feel my own training practice is subsiding into a rut, I personally reach for a psychology book – sometimes a 'popular' paperback, sometimes a weightier tome.

Invariably I find something to think about and something to use, even when I have disagreed completely with the author's views. I wish you also much enjoyment and much stimulation from a career-long relationship with psychology and psychologists. For that relationship can save you from knee-jerk reactions to training challenges (like putting on a video, or taking a coffee-break) and enable you to apply in practice what should perhaps be every trainer's motto:

If something isn't working, do something – anything – different!

References and Further Reading

BANDLER R and GRINDER J. (1982) *Frogs into Princes*. Utah, Real People Press.

BANDLER R and GRINDER J. (1982) *Reframing – Neurolinguistic Programming and the Transformation of Meaning*. Utah, Real People Press.

BETTELHEIM B. (1991) *The Informed Heart*. London, Penguin.

BION W R. (1961) *Experiences in Groups*. London, Tavistock Publications.

BRIGGS-MYERS I. (1980) *Gifts Differing*. California, Consulting Psychologists Press.

CADE B and O'HANLON W. (1993) *A Brief Guide to Brief Therapy*. London, Norton.

COOPER C L and MARSHALL J. (1978) *Understanding Executive Stress*. London, Macmillan.

COOPER C. (1995) *Psychology for Managers*. London, BPS and Macmillan Publishers Ltd.

DAVISON G C and NEALE J M. (1974) *Abnormal Psychology: An Experimental Clinical Approach*. Chichester, John Wiley and Sons.

ENGLER B. (1985) *Personality Theories*. London, Houghton Mifflin Company.

GEOGE E, IVESON C and RATNER H. (1990) *Problem to Solution: Brief Therapy with Individuals and Families*. London, BT Press.

GRAY J. (1971) *The Psychology of Fear and Stress.* London, Weidenfeld and Nicolson.

HARDINGHAM A. (1996) *Designing Training.* London, IPD.

HARDINGHAM A. (1995) *Working in Teams.* London, IPD.

HARRIS T. (1995) *I'm OK, You're OK.* London, Arrow Books.

HONEY P and MUMFORD A. (1995) *Using your Learning Styles.* Maidenhead, Honey.

KROEGER O and THUESEN J M. (1992) *Type Talk at Work.* New York, Delacorte Press.

MACKINTOSH N J and COLMAN A M (eds). (1994) *Learning and Skills.* London, Longman.

MINUCHIN S and FISHMAN H C. (1981) *Family Therapy Techniques.* London, Harvard University Press.

NELSON-JONES R. (1983) *Practical Counselling Skills.* London, Holt, Rinehart and Winston.

O'CONNOR J and MCDERMOTT I. (1996) *Principles of NLP.* London, Thorsons.

O'CONNOR J and MCDERMOTT I. (1997) *The Art of Systems Thinking.* London, Thorsons.

ROGERS C R. (1951) *Client-Centred Therapy.* London, Constable and Company.

SATIR V. (1978) *Conjoint Family Therapy.* London, Souvenir Press.

SCHUTZ W. (1958) *FIRO: A Three-Dimensional Theory of Interpersonal Behaviour.* London, Will Schutz Associates.

SENGE P. (1994) *The Fifth Discipline Fieldbook.* London, Nicholas Brealey Publishing.

STRACHEY J. (1953–66) *The Standard Edition of the Complete Psychological Works of Sigmund Freud, Volumes 1-24.* London, The Hogarth Press and the Institute of Psychoanalysis.

Index

attention and attention spans 37, 39–47, 51, 144
    factors affecting 46–7
aversion therapy 163

behaviourism and behaviourists 63, 68, 140–143, 163
behaviour therapy/therapies 162–4
Berne, Eric 122–8
body language 15
brain, functions within the 49–51
    right- and left- 50–51, 52
brief therapy *see* counselling

Cattell, James M. 30, 31
central nervous system 47–51
change *see* commitment to change/growth
cognitive approaches to learning *see* learning, cognitive
approaches to
cognitive aspects of personality 20
commitment to change/growth 53–71, 98, 105, 136
    barriers to 55
conditioned responses/conditioning 139, 140, 141,
    150–151
    operant conditioning 163
confidence, need of a trainer for 14
confidentiality in training 110–111
conflict in training 114–134, 153
    constructive use of 114, 115–117, 118
    Freudian theory on 120–122

left-hand column technique 131–3
personal reactions to 118–133
reframing 115–117, 129–130
transactional analysis of 122–8, 131
counselling 60, 61, 93–113, 154
constructive feedback 106–9, 111, 113
contrast with training 96–8, 100–102, 104, 106, 108,
111, 112, 113, 154
different approaches to 99–100, 104–9, 113
ethical issues of 109–112, 113
exception-finding 105
Johari window, the 106, 107–9, 113
'role counselling' 94
solution-focused brief therapy 104–6, 113
see also person-centred counselling; redundancy
counselling
credibility of trainer 9–11, 18, 19, 33, 36, 44, 83
curious/exploratory disposition 6, 8, 61, 126, 129

desensitisation 162, 163
discussion as a training tool 35
dislike of a person 11

ego, the 68, 120–122, 123, 127
emotions 55–6, 119, 153, 154, 155, 156, 158, 163
energy, as indication of rapport 9
excellence, the psychology of see neurolinguistic
programming

feedback see counselling; listening as training tool
'flooding' 163
Freudian theory see psychoanalysis and psychoanalysts
funnel, the see questioning as training tool

group dynamics 72–92, 114
Bion's theory of group working 84–9, 90, 92
conformity 81–3, 92, 95
encounter groups 89–91, 92
groupthink 83

Schutz's psychodynamic theory of group working 76–80, 92
group training 72–92
    affection issues 79–80, 90
    bad experiences 73–6, 87–8, 91
    control issues 77–9, 80

Hawthorne effect, the 150
human information processor *see* perception, the psychology of
humour 9

id, the 120–122, 123
informing/getting information across 35–52
    signs of failure in 36–7
    with maximum impact 41–7
introduction techniques 77, 78
irrational fears 162

job satisfaction, increased 135
Johari window, the *see* counselling
Jung, Carl G. 20–24

Kolb's learning cycle *see* learning, Kolb's cycle of

'leading' after achieving rapport 15, 17–18, 33
learner-centred training/learning 53, 60
learning
    Bloom's hierarchical taxonomy of 147–8
    by association 139–141, 147, 150, 163
    classical theory of 138–143, 147, 150
    cognitive approaches to 143–9, 150–151
    context-specific 146
    Hawthorne effect, the 150
    Kolb's cycle of 148–9
    learner-centred 53, 60
    facilitating transfer of 135–151
    reinforcement of 140–143, 153, 163

rewards and punishments *see* conditioned responses/
    conditioning
learning disposition 6, 7–8, 11, 120, 137
learning theory, classical 138–143, 147, 150
life positions, the four *see* transactional analysis
listening as training tool 100, 102–3, 112–113
    exception-finding 105
    feedback 106–9, 111, 113
    reflecting and summarising 103
logical levels 14, 15

managing a training group 72–92
memory 120, 144, 156
    primacy and recency effects 42–4, 52
    research into long-term 143–9
    short-term 39, 40, 41–4, 51, 144
metamirror *see* neurolinguistic programming
mimicry 17
mind, complexity of the human 4–5, 6–7, 39, 52
'moments of truth' 62
motivation, the psychology of 53–63, 70, 158
    Herzberg's two-factor theory 59–60
    Maslow's hierarchy of human needs 56–9, 60
    Rogers' conditions for personal growth 60–63
Myers-Briggs Type Indicator (MBTI) questionnaire 20,
    23, 32, 40

neurolinguistic programming (NLP) 11–18, 33, 100,
    128–130, 133
    as the psychology of excellence 12, 33
    metamirror 128–9, 131
    reframing 115–117, 129–130
neurophysiology of the central nervous system 47–51,
    52
neurosis/neuroses 96, 97, 160–164, 167
    rational-emotive therapy 160–161

operant conditioning 163

'pacing' to achieve rapport 15–18, 33, 44, 103
Pavlov's conditioning experiment 139
people-focused disposition 2, 3, 6–7, 8
    as indication of rapport 9
perception, the psychology of 37–40, 45, 51, 120, 144
    the human information processor 39, 47–51, 52
personality theory 18–31, 33–4, 121
    Cattell's psychometric trait (16PF) theory 30–31
    Freudian concept of 121
    Jung's four-dimensional framework 20–23, 24–7
    other frameworks and their relevance 27–30
    questionnaire for team effectiveness 24–7
    questionnaire on philosophical assumptions 29
person-centred counselling 60–61, 63
phobia(s) 162, 163
probing see questioning as training tool
productivity, increased organisational 135
psychoanalysis and psychoanalysts 68, 84, 96, 97, 104,
    107, 111, 118, 120–122, 133, 138, 158–9, 167
    Freudian theory 120–122, 138
    key concepts 85, 96, 97
psychological frame of mind 5–8, 168
psychometric tests 30–33
psychotherapy 63–4

questioning as training tool 100–102, 112–113
    precision or fuzzy 100–102, 113
questionnaires as training tools 20, 23, 30, 32–3, 59
    360-degree feedback 33

rapport, inner/internal 11–14, 33
    effects of lack of 12–13, 17
rapport between trainer and trainees 9–10, 15–34, 83
    building 10, 11, 13, 14, 15–17, 18, 19, 23, 28, 33, 36
    indications of lack of 9–10
    see also 'leading'; 'pacing'
rational-emotive therapy 160–161
redundancy counselling 12–13, 14, 58
reframing to change perceptions 115–117, 129–130, 133

relaxation techniques 99, 162, 163, 167
relaxed atmosphere 3, 11, 15, 73
rewards and punishments *see* learning, by association/
    reinforcement of
Rogers, Carl 60–62
role-plays, of appraisals 35

Schutz's psychodynamic theory of group working 76–80
    the FIRO-B questionnaire 76
self-actualisation 57–9, 60, 70
self-control 67–70, 71
self-disclosure in training 110, 111–112
Senge, Peter 131–3, 136
sensitivity to trainees' capacities 10, 37, 106–9, 127
seven, the magic number 38–40
Skinner, B. F. 27, 60, 140–141, 163
social psychology 118–119
split personalities, everybody as 11–13
stress and stress management 152–167
    sources of stress in training 165–6, 167
    stress profile(s) 164, 167
    stress-related illnesses 157, 165
    the physiology of stress 155–8, 167
summarising *see* listening as training tool
super-ego, the 120–122, 123
systems thinking/approaches 63–7, 68, 70, 130–134
    the individual as a system 64–6, 70
    the individual within many systems 66–7, 70–71

training evaluation 135
training programme(s)
    design of 1–4, 46–7, 61, 82
    with psychological input 3–5, 8, 28–9
    without psychological input 1–2, 5
transfer of learning *see* learning, facilitating transfer of
transactional analysis 12, 122–8, 131, 133
    the four life positions 126–8

vigilance tasks/studies 44–7
    the Cambridge Cockpit 45–6